A student's guide to Auditing

by Alan Lewin

KAPLAN

PUBLISHING

British library cataloguing-in-publication data
A catalogue record for this book is available from the British Library.
Published by:
Kaplan Publishing UK
Unit 2 The Business Centre
Molly Millars Lane
Wokingham
Berkshire
RG41 2QZ

ISBN 978-0-85732-203-6

© Alan Lewin

First edition published 2010

Printed and bound in Great Britain.

Contents

About this book

Why do you need this book?

The most common reason for students of auditing failing their exams is lack of understanding of what an audit is or why it is carried out. This happens either because the student has never actually been on an audit, or simply because learning about auditing is seen to be boring.... I've tried to change this...

This book is essential reading for students sitting auditing exams based on International Standards of Auditing. The target exam level is roughly comparable to ACCA Foundation Fundamentals Level, although it also provides a readable introduction to what those strange people called "auditors" do in a company.

As in any subject, auditing has some facts that must be understood. This book tries to help you understand those auditing facts in an easy to access form because:

- it provides practical examples of what happens on an audit using an example client

- it refers to Auditing Standards, but only to show how they relate to audits with some "Plain English" translation of the key points of the standard

- it is written in a student-friendly, down to earth, style

- it includes a revision chapter, summarising the main sections of the International Auditing Standards in an easy to revise format, and, best of all,

- it assumes no initial knowledge of auditing at all.

How to use this book

You can use this book in a number of ways:

1. as a general reading book to learn about auditing – which means that you will probably read it cover to cover

2. as a reference work to key points of an audit – dipping into the book as you need information on specific parts of an audit, or

3. as a revision aid to remind yourself about sections of an audit or Auditing Standards before taking an examination.

But, as long as you start to find auditing perhaps just a little bit interesting, I don't mind how you read it.

About the chapters

Most books about auditing jump straight into detailing the applicable theory, quoting from the Auditing Standards and then provide very detailed written examples of how that theory works. This book deliberately avoids this approach. Each chapter starts with an introduction explaining what you will learn, and for many chapters, an overview or roadmap of the key sections.

The chapters then explain the different sections of an audit, using icons to identify key points. Those icons are as follows:

 **Example**

To ensure an understanding of each section of an audit, most chapters include an example of an audit "in action" as it were, using a book distributor as a case study. See below for an introduction to our "client".

 **Definitions**

These can't be avoided. Many auditing standards contain key definitions; these are included in the text to show how that definition relates to a real audit.

key "need to learn" bit

If you are facing a closed book examination, it will not be enough just to be comfortable with the subject matter and to feel you understand an issue – there are some key "need to learn" bits for each Standard. You will, therefore, have to commit some key issues to memory. These are highlighted for you as you work through a topic.

 **Memory devices**

These are ideas to help you remember the very interesting and most important parts of an audit and the Auditing Standards. They could be an acronym, mnemonic or similar technique. Remember, however, that many learners will benefit from constructing their own diagrams or creating their own mnemonics. How I remember things may not be the way you remember things.

In summary, the icons in the book mean:

 Example

 Definitions

 Key "need to learn" bit

 Memory devices

Our client

The example client used in this book is called 27/4Books. This company is a book wholesaler – that is they purchase books from publishers and then sell the books on, mainly to bookshops where members of the public can buy those books. They have been around for a few years and require a statutory audit.

27/4Books is run by a board of directors, but is owned by its shareholders. It is correctly incorporated under the company legislation in its home country.

The company's most recent Income Statement and Statement of Financial Position are shown below. The icons beside many of the figures on the Statement of Financial Position will be used later to guide you through the audit of 27/4Books.

27/4Books Ltd Income Statement		
	52 Weeks ended 30 Dec 20X1 $'000	52 Weeks ended 31 Dec 20X0 $'000
Sales	11,023	9,557
Cost of Sales	7,923	6,217
Gross profit	3,100	3,340
Administration costs	1,602	1,557
Selling and distribution costs	1,221	1,524
Net profit before taxation	277	259
Taxation	95	87
Net profit after taxation	182	172

27/4Books

Statement of Financial Position – 31 December 20X1

	20X1 $'000	20X0 $'000	Icon
Non-current assets	653	698	
Current assets			
Inventory	2,055	1,943	
Receivables	1,753	1,525	
Prepayments	56	50	
Cash and bank	489	506	
Total current assets	**4,353**	**4,024**	
Current liabilities			
Payables	982	886	
Accruals	101	95	
Total current liabilities	1,083	981	
Net current assets	3,270	3,043	
Total net assets	**3,923**	**3,741**	
Shareholders' funds			
Share capital	500	500	
Reserves	3,423	3,241	
Total shareholders' funds	**3,923**	**3,741**	

I'll refer back to this SFP during explanation of the audit procedures later in this book.

As you can see, the company is profitable with a net profit after taxation of $182,000. However, although sales have increased, gross profit is falling (down to $3,100,000); the only reason profit increased this year appears to have been the large decrease in distribution costs (down to $1,221,000). Sorry, I'm thinking like an auditor already – but there again if you looked at the Income Statement and thought similar thoughts you're well on the way to being an auditor also.

What do you notice about the Statement of Financial Position? The company has significant reserves ($3,423,000) quite a lot of cash ($489,000) and overall net assets. This means that the audit assignment won't be too risky – but we'll find out more later in the book.

Assume we have been appointed auditor for this financial year – and we'll work through the audit of this company as we progress through the book.

And finally:

My "thank you" bit. My grateful thanks to:

- my publisher – for the idea and support during the writing process

- my reviewer Andy Bradley – for the independent view and many helpful suggestions

- my typesetting team – just wait until you see the pictures they came up with...

- everyone else who has assisted with the project (my family, friends and students...).

Of course, in my opinion, this book is true and fair, however, any errors are mine.

Chapter 1
Why auditors?

A student's guide to Auditing By Alan Lewin

1.1 Introduction – what will you learn?

This chapter explains why auditors are mis-understood and shows the value of audits, initially in a personal, and then in a business context.

1.2 So, what is in this chapter?

Specifically this chapter covers:

- the basic question of why we have auditors

- why auditors are necessary as independent checkers, both in a personal context (selling a motor vehicle) and in a company context (auditing financial statements).

To start with, let's ask the big question....

1.3 Introduction – why do we have auditors?

Be honest – and answer the question "why do we have auditors?"

- If you work in an organisation that has been the subject of an audit, then the auditors appear each year and generally make a nuisance of themselves requesting all sorts of documents and asking lots of questions. So, "why do we have auditors?" probably gets a fairly impolite answer along the lines of "no idea – they just waste my time!".

- If you work in a firm providing audit services, then you visit lots of different organisations each year to perform the audit. Your training has hopefully explained the reason for the audit, but the potentially boring work and the possible lack of helpfulness within the organisation may make you slightly "jaundiced" in your outlook. So, "why do we have auditors?" probably means something like "well it's a job and I get paid".

- If you are a shareholder in an organisation, then you will receive a report from the auditors on each set of financial statements. The report doesn't say that much (normally less than one page) while the audit work takes months; you may be concerned about the actual value of the report. So "why do we have auditors?" may get the response "I think they help me but their report isn't half expensive".

- If you are a general member of society (that is you, me, the next person you see in the street etc), then you generally hear about auditors only when something goes wrong within an organisation (such as Enron) which the auditor failed to identify and report on. So "why do we have auditors?" may get the response "no idea – they are overpaid and don't help to stop problems in companies anyway – why bother with them?"

Ok, auditors get bad press perhaps due to lack of understanding and because their work is largely "secret" and is not seen by most people.

1.4 Change the scenario

So, let's change the scenario.

You want to buy a second hand (or used) car. What do you do?

You see this advert in the local paper. You've always wanted an Austin Midi (your favourite car); the price looks right, so you phone Alan, arrange to see the car, like it and buy it. Just like that??

You could, but surely you've placed a lot of trust in Alan that the car is in-fact of low mileage, mechanically sound etc. especially if you know nothing about cars (apart from being able to drive one).

What else could you do?

- Try driving the car, but this will only show you the car works "now".

- Inspect the car for "obvious" defects – but if Alan is clever, any defects won't be "obvious" to the untrained eye.

- Ask a friend to inspect the car –but again your friend may not have any detailed knowledge of cars.

OR ask a specialist to check the car for you. In other words ask someone with knowledge of cars to actually test the car to ensure that it is mechanically "as new" and not about to fall to bits as soon as you pay your $876 and drive it away.

Good, you've just employed an auditor!

Just a minute

No, that's what auditors do – they use their skill and knowledge to "check" things such as company financial statements for people who don't have the skill (or time) to do that for themselves. In the same way that you want assurance that the car of your dreams is really roadworthy, shareholders of companies want assurance that the financial statements produced by that company are correct.

Convinced? OK, perhaps not quite yet so let's look at the purchase of the car in more detail.

USED AUSTIN MIDI FOR SALE

- Dark blue
- Low mileage
- Mechanically "as new"
- One careful owner
- Includes road tax to end of year

$876

Contact **Alan** on **0020052865**

1.5 Work of an auditor (1) - Buying a car

Follow the steps below regarding the purchase of the car in this diagram.

MOT
TEST CERTIFICATE

REPORT

Qualified

3

5

4

6

PROSPECTIVE BUYER

SKILLED MECHANIC

CURRENT OWNER

1

2

Activity		Commentary

1  A crocodile has a bright idea of buying a second hand car. This car is currently owned by what appears to be a relatively juvenile man in a suit – can he be trusted?

2  The buyer asks a skilled mechanic to check the car to make sure it is safe, roadworthy etc. The expert is called in because the buyer does not have the time or skill to check the car.

3 The buyer knows that the skilled mechanic will do a good job for two reasons – firstly because the mechanic will apply some standard of safety (such as the MOT test in the UK) to the car, ensuring that the car meets that standard.

4  Secondly, the mechanic is qualified from an appropriate society or institution – he therefore knows how to ensure that the car is safe and that the amount of money being asked by the vendor is reasonable.

5 The mechanic produces a report on the car which is given to the buyer. The report explains whether or not the car is safe and may recommend a purchase price.

6 The buyer should be happy because there is now an independent opinion on whether the car is safe and worth the purchase price. However, the buyer has made the implicit assumption that the mechanic and the current owner are not related to each other. If this was the case then the mechanic could be tempted to provide an incorrect report to "help" his relation.

More on the ethics of auditing in Chapter 2.

So that's all there is to buying a car. The buyer employs an expert to provide a report on whether the car is safe and that the purchase price is reasonable. Now compare this with an audit on the financial statements of an organisation.

1.6 Work of an auditor (2) – auditing company financial statements

Here's the same diagram but with some different elements. You own shares in a company, but in common with many shareholders, you don't actually run the company. The company is run by the directors; they make the management decisions, invest company money, decide what products to sell and who to employ etc. Finally the directors give back to you, and all other shareholders, a report on how much money (or profit) the company has made. This enables you to make an informed decision on whether or not to continue your investment in the company, that is sell your shares, or even buy more shares if you think that the prospects for the company are good.

But how do you know that the report (that is the financial statements) are actually correct and not simply something that the directors have made up? This would involve reviewing the whole accounting system in your company, something you don't have the time or skills to actually do. So, what you do is employ an auditor to do that checking for you.

So, follow the diagram and explanation below to find out what happens on an audit.

Activity

1

2

Stater...

3

INTERNATIONAL STANDARDS ON AUDITING

The auditor carries out an ...
Standards on Auditing. These are inter...
agreed standards on how an audit should be
performed which literally set the standard of work
that an auditor will follow.

4

Qualified

The auditor is a qualified accountant which means
he or she has the skills to carry out the audit.

5

AUDITOR'S REPORT TO THE MEMBERS OF ...

The auditor produces a report on the financial
statements which is given to the shareholders.
The report explains whether the financial
statements are "correct", that is show a true and
fair view. See chapter 9 for more detail on how to
understand audit reports.

6

The shareholders should be happy because they
now have an independent opinion concerning the
accuracy of the financial statements. However,
they have assumed that the directors preparing
the financial statements and the auditor and not
related to each other. But again that's an ethical
issue for the next chapter...

So that's all there is to an audit. The shareholder employs an expert to provide a report
on whether the financial statements are correct. This means that they can make an
informed decision on whether or not to continue investing in the company. The auditor
provides "credibility" to the financial statements.

1.7 Why do we have auditors

Key point	Further discussion
We have auditors because they "check" or audit financial statements to ensure that those statements are correct. The auditor is employed because shareholders do not have the time or skills to perform the audit themselves.	
Auditors carry out their work in accordance with a given standard (the International Standards on Auditing (ISA)) which means that the standard of work is known.	See chapter 2 for an outline of the standards and chapters 4 to 9 to see how those standards are applied in the work of an auditor.
Auditors have a professional qualification which means they have shown that they have the knowledge to carry out an audit, and will ensure ethically that work is placed before their own interests.	See chapter 2 for a discussion of how ethics applies to auditors.
Auditors will then prepare a report in an agreed format making it easy to identify when they have concerns about the items being audited.	See chapter 9 for a explanation of auditors' reports.

1.8 Chapter summary

Hopefully you can now see the value of having auditors. They provide a helpful service by attempting to ensure that company financial statements are correct. In the next chapter we look at pressures on auditors which could mean the audit report may not be trusted.

1.9 Summary of the summary

Here's the chapter in just 21 words.

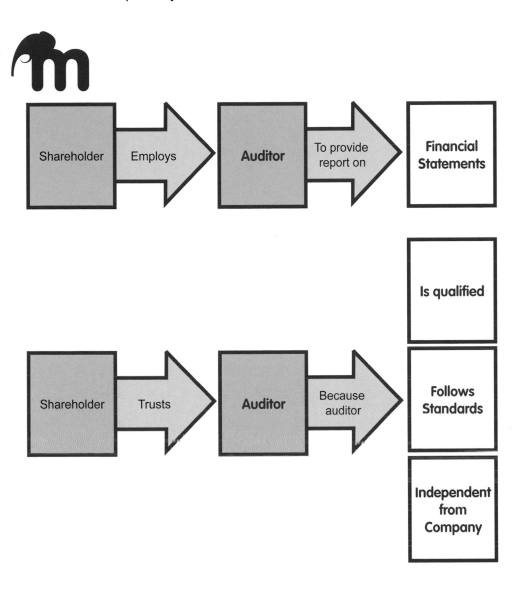

And if you counted the words you're well on the way to being an auditor...

Chapter 2
Why trust an auditor?

2.1 Introduction – what will you learn?

This chapter explains the ethical framework that surrounds the work of an auditor.   By the end of the chapter you should have no doubts at all about trusting an auditor!

2.2 So, what is in this chapter?

Specifically this chapter covers:

- the ethical framework within which auditors work

- the fundamental ethical principles that auditors must follow

- the conceptual framework which provides various defences to ensure ethical principles are followed

- specific threats to ethical principles

- an introduction to the ISAs including a quick summary of the current list.

2.3 Introduction to the ethical framework

The accounting profession looks on auditors in exactly the same way as you view your doctor. There are threats (or diseases) which are always trying to attack you. This means that defences are needed to avoid either catching those diseases – or if you suspect you are ill, to remove the disease as quickly as possible.

In fact, there are layers of ethics that auditors must follow to try and avoid "disease" in our example.

Firstly, there are the five fundamental principles that every auditors must follow.

Secondly, a conceptual framework and a series of safeguards exist to avoid breaking the principles, and to protect the auditors from the threats which try and pull the auditors away from doing the "right" thing.

As a roadmap, here's our star auditors with the five fundamental principles, being protected by the safeguards from the threats trying to compromise his or her principles.

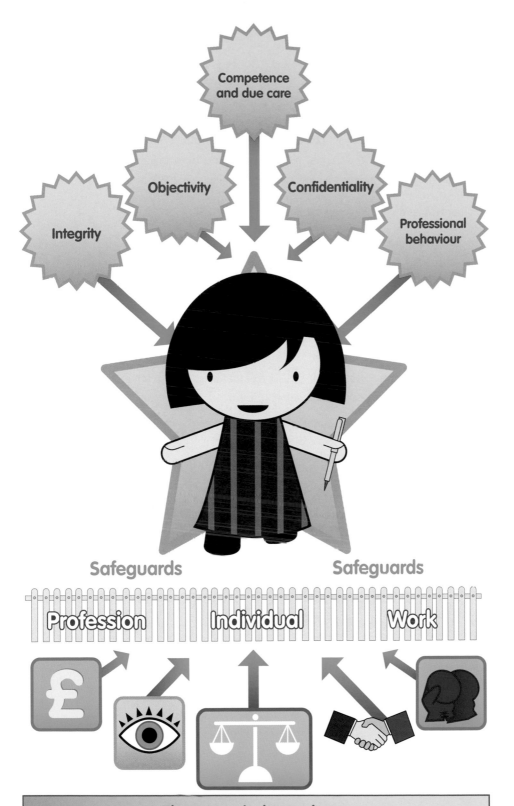

Let's see how this works in practice.

2.4 Things that must always be done.

The fundamental principles are really key qualities you expect of any auditors. In fact the qualities you expect in an auditors are the same as you expect when seeing your doctor. When you feel ill, you expect an honest assessment of your illness and an accurate diagnosis. You also don't expect your doctor to be incompetent or to discuss your health issues with anyone else (unless you give permission).

In other words, qualities of your auditor are:

Fundamental principle	Example
Integrity — Integrity	
A professional auditor should be straightforward and honest in all professional and business relationships.	If an auditor says something can be done, or that the fee is so much, then that is the truth.
Objectivity — Objectivity	
A professional auditor should not allow bias, conflict of interest or undue influence of others to override professional or business judgments.	An auditor provides an honest report which can be trusted. There is no bias (real or perceived) in making the report (see below for potential areas of bias).

Competence and due care **Fundamental principle**	**Example**
Professional Competence and Due Care	
A professional auditor has a continuing duty to maintain professional knowledge and skill at the level required to ensure that a client or employer receives competent professional service based on current developments in practice, legislation and techniques. A professional auditor should act diligently and in accordance with applicable technical and professional standards when providing professional services.	Passing examinations is, initially, how auditors show they have knowledge of auditing. However, auditors also have to keep "up-to-date" – hence the Continued Professional Development requirement. Also, auditors report using a common set of rules or principles, (that is the ISAs as discussed below) so the standard of work is clearly understood.
Confidentiality **Confidentiality**	
A professional auditor should respect the confidentiality of information acquired as a result of professional and business relationships and should not disclose any such information to third parties without proper and specific authority unless there is a legal or professional right or duty to disclose. Confidential information acquired as a result of professional and business relationships should not be used for the personal advantage of the professional auditor or third parties.	Auditors do not pass on information gained from or about clients without good reason. As in the patient / doctor relationship, information provided to the auditor stays there unless an action like a court order means that the information must be disclosed.

Fundamental principle	Example
Professional Behaviour	
A professional auditor should comply with relevant laws and regulations and should avoid any action that discredits the profession.	The auditor is not a lawbreaker, but shows acceptance of society, is a good member of society, by following the laws of society.

Of course, the principles are simply that, a set of guidelines. This means that each individual auditor could, in theory, interpret those guidelines differently. The guidelines are therefore enforced with the conceptual framework.

2.5 Avoid doing harm (the conceptual framework)

The "conceptual framework" recognises that there are many reasons why auditors may appear not to be trustworthy. Furthermore, it is impossible to list out every reason. So, auditors must be "on the lookout" for any "threats" which appear to suggest that the auditor is not acting "correctly".

The conceptual framework always works in this way:

so, follow the diagram and explanation below to find out what happens on an audit.

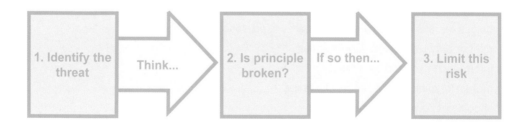

Firstly, identify the threat that will cause a fundamental principle to be broken.

Secondly, decide how likely it is that the fundamental principle will be broken.

Lastly, and where the threat is more than negligible, decide on ways of limiting the risk that the principle will be broken.

2.6 Application of the conceptual framework

In other words, let's say you have just painted the fence around your house which also borders a public footpath. It is important that people do not touch the fence until the paint is dry, or their skin or clothes will become stained with the paint. Assume also that there is a general principle in society that one member does not allow harm to come to other members if it can possibly be avoided.

This means in terms of fence painting and the principles:

Conceptual framework	Painting a fence
1. Identify the threat	
Identify, evaluate and address threats to compliance with the fundamental principles.	There is a threat to the fundamental principle of not doing harm to other people in society.
2. Will a fundamental principle be broken?	
Identify, evaluate and respond to threats to compliance with the fundamental principles.	The threat is relatively severe, lots of people walk along the path by your fence.
3. Limit the risk of breaking the fundamental principle	
Apply safeguards to eliminate the threats or reduce them to an acceptable level, such that compliance with the fundamental principles is not compromised.	You try and reduce the threat by putting up signs saying "wet paint – do not touch" to warn people that the paint is wet. This limits the potential harm to people in society.

2.7 Safeguards in the conceptual frameworks

In this context, safeguards are things which try to reduce threats to an acceptable level. For auditors there are three groups of safeguards created by:

Each of these is discussed below. Each section shows the following:

Title of the safeguard from the auditor's ethical guidance	Explanation of the safeguard	Example of the safeguard

Safeguards created by the Profession

	These are regulations which effectively force auditors to work in specific ways.	

Safeguard	What is the safeguard?	Example
Education and training prior to becoming a qualified auditor.	Potential audit professionals (aka you the student) are required to show understanding of ethical matters and gain knowledge avoiding ethical conflicts.	Passing professional examinations and gaining experience at work prior to taking part in assurance engagements.
Continuing Professional Education or Development (CPD).	Methods of ensuring that the audit professional refresh and update their knowledge of ethics etc over time.	Undertaking CPD relevant to the assurance professional's work.
Legislation.	Country based legislation enforcing important ethical safeguards.	In the UK, Companies Acts legislation stating who can, and cannot, be an auditor.
Corporate governance regulations.	Country based guidance (with some international guidance) setting out best practice for some ethical situations.	In the UK, the Combined Code of the stock exchange and internationally the COSO guidance suggest appropriate procedures for some assurance work.

Safeguards created by the

Activities that the individual auditor can do to limit the ethical threats.

Safeguard	What is the safeguard?	Example
Complying with CPD regulations.	Staying up-to-date with current legislation and other knowledge needed to perform professional work.	An auditor will read and understand new auditing standards.
Keeping in contact with other professionals including auditors, legal advisors and professional bodies.	The auditor can discuss informally potential problems, with similar professional people.	Contacting the ethics department at the auditor's professional Institute (e.g. the ACCA) for guidance on specific ethical threats.
Using an independent mentor.	Having a formal relationship with another auditor to discuss ethical threats.	Having nominated individuals in each auditing firm available to discuss ethical threats on a confidential basis.

Safeguards at

These are work methods designed to try and ensure that ethical threats do not occur.

Safeguard	What is the safeguard?	Example
Firm-wide standards which will be obtained from professional codes of ethics all audit firms will follow. These ethical codes are outside the scope of this book.	Controls and procedures with the audit firm to ensure that all members of that firm are not subject to ethical threats.	Setting the "tone" of the audit firm by partners being seen to follow ethical rules, down to review of work and documented internal procedures that all staff are required to follow.

Ethical standards relating to audit engagements - again these standards are outside the scope of this book.	Controls designed to ensure that each assurance assignment is completed with no ethical threats being found.	Include review of work carried out, discussing potential threats with independent parties including those charged with governance (such as the audit committee) and rotating assurance staff regularly.

That is the general way to mitigate threats. However, ethical codes also identifies five specific threats and provides guidance on how to mitigate them.

2.8 Specific threats

Here are the specific threats – with an explanation of each threat and an example of how the threat can be decreased (or mitigated in the terminology of the ethical codes).

Self-interest threats

Conflict between the personal interests of the auditor and the client; the auditor is tempted to obtain personal benefit (or benefit a close family member) rather than provide an appropriate service for the client.

Threat	Why is this a threat	How to mitigate?
Holding shares in a client (financial interest).	Auditor wants to protect that investment – an adverse audit report could decrease the value of shares.	Don't hold any financial interests.
Obtain significant income from one client.	Auditor will not want to upset the client (for example by qualifying the audit report) for fear of losing those fees.	Limit the amount of income generated from one client (for example, 10% of total fee income for listed companies and 15% of total fee income for other companies).

Working with a client in other ways such as a separate business venture.	Auditor may want the (successful) business venture to continue and not prejudice this by issuing a qualified report on the client's accounts.	Don't have any other business ventures with a client.
Providing a client with a loan (this can include unpaid audit fees).	Auditor may be concerned that a qualified audit report may jeopardise the loan repayment.	Don't make (or receive) any loans.

Self-review threats

The auditor prepares a document, and then has to review that document for errors. Most people don't see their own mistakes.

Example of threat	Why is this a threat	How to mitigate?
Reporting on systems or controls in a client when the auditor designed those controls for the client.	The auditor will not want to criticise his own work – hence potentially ignores any control weaknesses found.	Get another auditor not involved with design work to review – or simply don't carry out design work for client.
The auditor was, until recently, a director or officer at the client.	The auditor was involved in decision making / preparing documentation at the client; as an auditor they will not have an independent view of that documentation.	Wait some appropriate amount of time (such as two years) prior to actually being the auditor of the "ex" client.

Advocacy threats

The auditor is seen to be promoting or supporting the client in some way. The auditor's objectivity may be compromised because he believes he must always support the client.

Example of threat	Why is this a threat	How to mitigate?
Promoting (or supporting) a sale of shares for a client.	The auditor may be suggesting that the shares are a good investment – although the auditor is really taking no view on this matter.	Don't promote any sale of shares.
Support a client in court in a dispute with a third party.	The auditor will find it difficult to take an objective view because of other business relationships (that is client must be supported else the auditor could lose the audit).	Don't support the client in court.

Familiarity threats

The auditor gets too close or friendly with a client so actions may be biased to assisting that client; independent judgement is lost.

Example of threat	Why is this a threat	How to mitigate?
The auditor has a close family member working at an audit client.	The auditor may be biased to support that family member (by not reporting errors made by the person, for example).	Auditors cannot audit clients where close family members work.
The auditor accepts gifts from the client.	The gift could be seen as a bribe or attempt to influence the auditor.	Don't accept gifts (unless the value is negligible).
The auditor has been carrying out the audit of a client for a long period of time.	Over time the auditor loses independence as they become too familiar with the client. For example, the auditor may simply accept explanations rather than testing the accuracy of statements made.	Audit partners are rotated away from clients on a regular basis (normally between 5 and 7 years).

Intimidation threats

Situations where the auditor cannot act in an unbiased manner because of threats (physical or other) from the client.

Example of threat	Why is this a threat	How to mitigate?
The client threatens to dismiss the auditor if the accounts are qualified.	The auditor does not qualify the accounts when they should have been.	Make the correct ethical decision and qualify the accounts anyway.
The client threatens to sue the auditor for providing a poor standard of work unless other concessions are made.	The auditor doesn't want any bad publicity and so accepts whatever the client wants.	Always try and ensure that contracts with clients are fulfilled – no room then for the client to threaten poor work.
Client demands that the auditor reduce the audit fee, normally along with the amount of audit work carried out.	The amount of audit work will be insufficient to support the audit opinion (or an audit opinion cannot be given).	Explain to client the need for audit work. At the extreme, resign from carrying out the audit.

You will need to learn the ethical guidance and examples as shown above. Many many examination questions are built around scenarios which will include ethical threats facing an auditor. These threats will have to be identified, explained and an appropriate method of mitigation suggested. To be fair, most questions use the specific threats above to provide these precise examples.

2.9 Standards to be followed

Auditors have to follow rules. Hopefully you recall from chapter 1 that we gained confidence our garage mechanic gave a correct report on the car because a standard set of rules for checking the car was being followed. Here is the introduction to the rules for auditing.

These rules are called the International Standards on Auditing (or ISAs) – not to be confused with International Accounting Standards (IASs). Each standard focuses on one specific audit area and states what an audit shall do to comply with that standard. The use of the word shall is important. The ISAs were revised in 2008/09 to use common wording – with shall being the word to show what auditors effectively must do to comply with each standard.

Each standard follows a set format, with some words in **bold** text. These words are the standard itself; words in normal text provide an explanation of how the standard is to be applied.

This section provides a list of the standards in issue. I've given you an overview (in the key point column) to state what the standard does, and then a chapter reference in this book to where the standard is explained in more detail. No chapter reference means that the standard is specialised and knowledge of it is not needed for a basic understanding of auditing.

As you will see, the ISAs are split into groups; this grouping is followed below.

 Treat this section as a reference document – and as an alternative index to discover where each standard is explained in this book.

2.10 Introducing the ISAs

200 – 299 General principles and responsibilities

These standards set out the overall framework for audit engagements including the contract for the engagement (ISA 210) and methods of reporting to the client (ISA 260).

Number	Title	Key point	Chapter reference
200	Overall objectives of the independent auditor and the conduct of an audit in accordance with International Standards on Auditing.	Provides guidance on the overall objective of auditing financial statements – the overall objective is that the auditor must be able to give an audit opinion on whether financial statements are prepared in accordance with applicable reporting standards.	4.3
210	Agreeing the terms of audit engagements.	Sets out the standard contents of the engagement letter (contract between the auditor and the client) and when the letter should be issued and revised.	4.4

Number	Title	Key point	Chapter reference
220	Quality control for an audit of financial statements.	Provides guidance on the quality control procedures that are to be used on audits.	5.4 and 8.8
230	Audit documentation.	Provides guidance on audit documentation to be produced and sets standards that the documentation should follow.	5.10
240	The auditor's responsibility relating to fraud in an audit of financial statements.	Explains fraud and error and the respective duties of auditors and management in detecting and preventing fraud and error.	4.9
250	Consideration of laws and regulations in an audit of financial statements.	In this ISA, the laws and regulations are those which the entity being audited must comply with. The ISA provides guidance on how the auditor can assess compliance with those laws and regulations.	Not covered directly
260	Communication with those charged with governance.	Explains how to identify persons "charged with governance" and the information to be communicated to those persons.	Not covered directly
265	Communicating deficiencies in internal control to those charged with governance and management.	How to write a letter explaining control weaknesses found during an audit.	8.7

300 – 499 Risk assessment and response to assessed risks

Explain how to plan the audit to identify potential problem areas (that is risks).

Number	Title	Key point	Chapter reference
300	Planning and audit of financial statements.	Explains how an auditor develops first an audit strategy and then an audit plan to ensure that the audit is performed in an effective manner.	4.5
315	Identifying and assessing the risks of material misstatement through understanding the entity and its environment.	Builds on ISA 200 to explain the information needed to assess the risk of material misstatement in the financial statements.	4.6

Number	Title	Key point	Chapter reference
320	Materiality in planning and performing an audit.	Provides guidance on what materiality is and how determination of materiality is used to help assess audit risk.	5.5
330	The auditor's responses to assessed risks.	Builds on ISA 315 to explain the work the auditor carries out when the risk of material misstatement is high (from ISA 320).	5.6
402	Audit considerations relating to an entity using service organisations.	Explains how to place reliance on service organisations (third parties providing accounting and other services to an audit client). Quite specialised and not covered in this book.	n/a
450	Evaluation of misstatements identified during the audit.	Explains how to understand the extent of misstatements found during the audit.	8.5

500 – 599 Audit Evidence

Explain what audit evidence is and the normal evidence that will be collected in various situations.

Number	Title	Key point	Chapter reference
500	Audit evidence.	Provides guidance on how the auditor can collect sufficient appropriate audit evidence from which reasonable conclusions can be drawn to support the opinion on the financial statements.	5.7
501	Audit evidence – specific considerations for selected items.	Supports ISA 500 by providing more guidance on the audit of some specific audit areas including counting physical inventory.	7.10

Number	Title	Key point	Chapter reference
505	External confirmations.	Explains the use of external confirmations (obtaining audit evidence from third parties) in decreasing audit risk.	7.8, 7.11 and 7.13
510	Initial audit engagements – opening balances.	Provides guidance on the audit of opening balances (the trial balance at the beginning of the year) where these figures have not been audited by the current auditor.	Not covered
520	Analytical procedures.	Explains how and when to use analytical procedures in an audit.	5.9
530	Audit sampling.	Assists in determining the selection of items for audit testing.	5.8
540	Auditing accounting estimates, including fair value accounting estimates, and related disclosures.	Provides guidance on the audit of accounting estimates – year-end balances where some judgement is involved in determining their value.	Not covered
550	Related parties.	Builds on IAS 24 (yes that is the accounting standard) explaining how to obtain evidence and ensure sufficient disclosure of these transactions in the financial statements.	5.12
560	Subsequent events.	Guidance on how events after the reporting date (subsequent events) may affect the financial statements.	8.3
570	Going concern.	Guidance on how to assess whether a company will continue to be in existence.	8.4
580	Written representations.	Provides guidance on when to obtain, and the key elements of, a management representation letter.	8.6

600 – 699 Using the work of others

How to place reliance on other firms of auditors, internal audit and experts.

Number	Title	Key point	Chapter reference
600	Special considerations - audits of group financial statements.	Guidance on using work of other auditors – for example where holding company and subsidiary company are audited by different firms of auditors. Specialist standard normally used only in group audit.	n/a
610	Using the work of internal auditors.	Explains how reliance for external audit purposes can be placed on work carried out by internal auditors.	5.13
620	Using the work of an auditor's expert.	Explains how reliance can be placed on experts where they provide evidence which an auditor cannot easily verify.	5.14

700 – 799 Audit conclusions and reporting

How to report the results of audit engagements to shareholders and other parties.

Number	Title	Key point	Chapter reference
700	Forming an opinion and reporting on financial statements.	Explains the format and content of a standard auditor's report.	9.3
705	Modifications to the opinion in the independent auditor's report.	Shows how a standard audit report is modified to draw attention to problems or possible mistakes in the financial statements.	9.6
706	Emphasis of matter paragraphs and other matter paragraphs in the independent auditor's report.	Explains how to bring matters to the attention of readers of the audit report – without qualifying that report.	9.5

Number	Title	Key point	Chapter reference
710	Comparative information - corresponding figures and comparative financial statements	Explains the auditor's work on comparative information in financial statements.	9.9
720	The auditor's responsibilities relating to other information in documents containing audited financial statements	Consideration of audit work necessary on other documents issued with financial statements (such as the annual report of a company).	9.10

2.11 Summary of the summary

A few more words this time – about 35 to be materially correct (see chapter 4 re materiality).

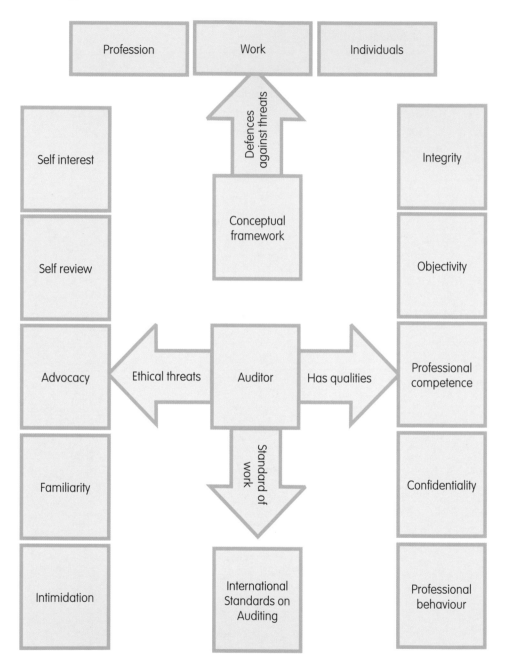

Chapter 3

The audit cycle

the legal bit

A student's guide to Auditing By Alan Lewin

3.1 Introduction – what will you learn?

This chapter explains the legal framework under which auditors operate, the duties they have and the power given to perform those duties.

To be fair, the precise duties and powers do vary by jurisdiction. Also, if you are taking an international examination such as ACCA, then there are relatively few questions on this area simply because duties and powers do vary. I have attempted to write this chapter to show the general duties and powers that auditors have in most jurisdictions. If you are taking an examination in a jurisdiction where specific knowledge of that country's legislation is required then you will need to enhance your studies in this area.

3.2 So, what is in this chapter?

Specifically this chapter covers:

- who can and cannot be an auditor

- how to appoint and remove an auditor from office

- what powers an auditor is given and what duties the auditor must perform

- the link between audit committees and external auditors

- who internal auditors are, and

- ISA 610 – Using the work of internal auditors.

3.3 Who can (and cannot) be an auditor

Can you be an auditor?

Each country will have its own rules - this is the situation in the United Kingdom.

Decision flowchart	Comment
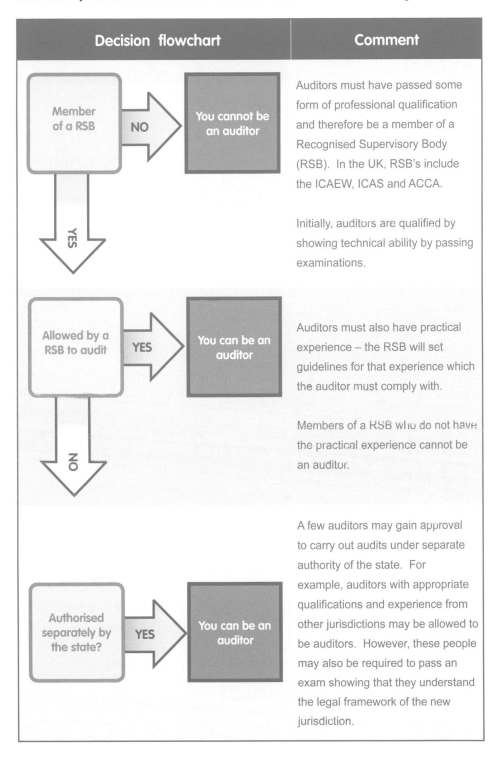	Auditors must have passed some form of professional qualification and therefore be a member of a Recognised Supervisory Body (RSB). In the UK, RSB's include the ICAEW, ICAS and ACCA. Initially, auditors are qualified by showing technical ability by passing examinations. Auditors must also have practical experience – the RSB will set guidelines for that experience which the auditor must comply with. Members of a RSB who do not have the practical experience cannot be an auditor. A few auditors may gain approval to carry out audits under separate authority of the state. For example, auditors with appropriate qualifications and experience from other jurisdictions may be allowed to be auditors. However, these people may also be required to pass an exam showing that they understand the legal framework of the new jurisdiction.

3.4 How to appoint (and lose) an auditor

Appointment

As a general rule auditors are appointed by the members, but there are a few exceptions, as shown below.

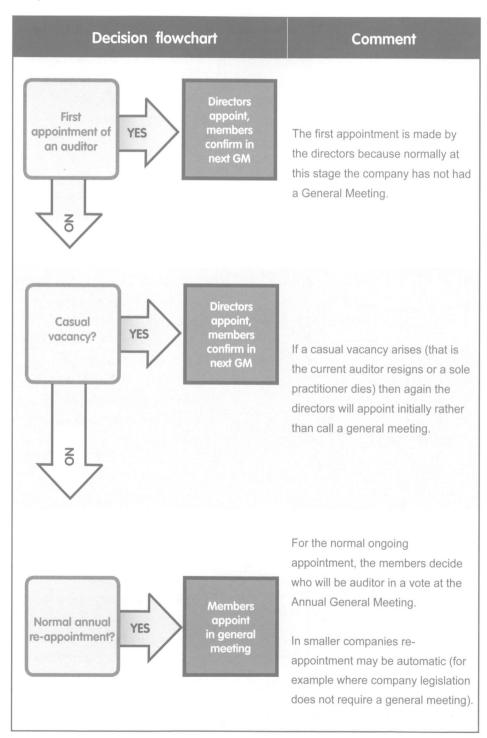

A normal term of office is from the end of the meeting where the auditor is appointed until the end of the next Annual General Meeting enabling the auditor to speak at that meeting about the audit of the financial statements presented at that meeting.

Losing an auditor

An auditor loses the job either by being removed (by the members) or by resigning.

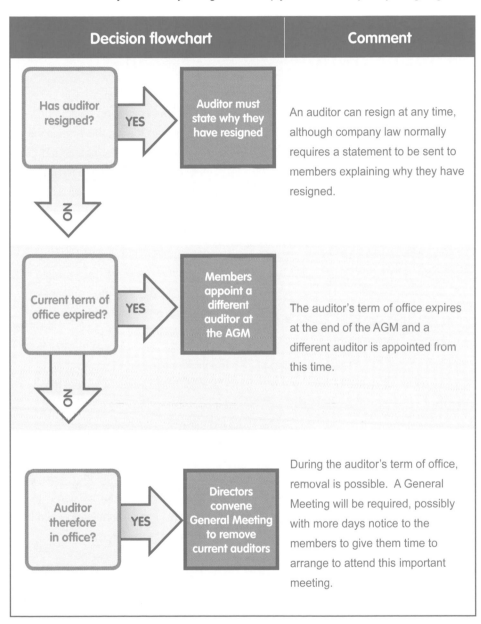

The most common reason for change in auditor is that the audit itself is put out to tender and a different audit firm provides a lower quote for the work. The auditor is then changed at the AGM as noted above.

3.5 Powers given to an auditor (rights of the job)

Without powers, the auditor would find it impossible to audit the financial statements and make a report as required by statute. Auditor's powers are normally provided by statute therefore to ensure that the statutory duties can be carried out.

Power	Reason for power
Access to the company's books and records at all reasonable times.	The auditor needs to see the company's books and records to audit them.
Receive all the information and explanations from company officials that the auditor considers are required for the audit.	The auditor has to form an opinion on the financial statements; this means the auditor decides what information and explanations are necessary to form that opinion. The directors are under a legal duty to provide that information and any explanations.
Receive notice of and be able to attend and speak at company meetings.	In some situations the auditor will want to speak to the members (for example to explain qualifications in their audit report). This power enables the auditor to make those comments.
Receive notice of and be able to attend any meeting proposing removal of the auditor.	If the auditor is being removed then the auditor may want to speak to the members to explain why the removal is not correct. This power enables the auditor to make those comments.
Upon resignation, the right to ask the directors to convene a general meeting.	If the auditor has to resign, then there are normally good reasons for making this decision. This power enables the auditor to tell the members of those reasons.

3.6 Things that the auditor must do (auditor's duties)

There are some things that an auditor must do (also called the auditor's duties). This section summarises those duties and explains the reason for them.

Duty	Reason for duty
Report to the company's members on whether or not the financial statements show a true and fair view.	The members need to know that the directors are running their (that is the members') company correctly. The financial statements provide a summary of that stewardship. The auditor effectively states that the directors' account of running the company is accurate (or not if the audit report is qualified – see chapter 9)
Report to the company's members on whether or not the financial statements have been properly prepared in accordance with relevant legislation.	There are laws that must be followed in preparing financial statements. The auditor confirms to the members that those rules have in fact been followed.
Report to the company's members (yes again) on any other matters required by company legislation – normally only if those matters have not been followed.	This is normally termed "reporting by exception"; the lack of any comment by the auditor means that certain things have happened. However, if these things have not happened, then the auditor will mention these in the report. See below for examples.
Report to the company's members on any other specific legislation.	Other reporting may be specific to individual countries.
To say why they are no longer the auditor of a company.	So that the members are aware of any reasons why the auditor resigned or why the auditor was removed from office. This is just in case the directors are trying to hide any reasons for changing an auditor.

3.7 Reporting by exception

In the UK an auditor must form an opinion on various matters (true and fair view etc) and state those in the audit report. However, there are a few other matters on which an opinion must be formed that only appear in the audit report if there are problems – matters reported on by exception.

So what does this mean – well this is just like a visit to the dentist – your dentist only tells you of problem teeth – not that most of your teeth are OK. In other words, your dentist reports by exception on your teeth, and in the same way the auditor reports by exception on a few other matters affecting a company.

You need to learn this list as it can form a basic factual question in an auditing examination.

Most auditing texts use the mnemonic RAPID to help remember these matters – I can't think of a better memory aid so this is used again here.

	Regulation	Explanation
R	Adequate **R**eturns have been received from branches not visited.	Some companies have many branches running similar accounting systems; rather than visit all the branches the auditor will visit a sample only. Audit evidence for the branches not visited is the returns (accounting records received) from those branches. If those returns were not adequate the auditor would state this in the audit report.
A	The **A**ccounting records are consistent with the financial statements.	This confirms that the financial statements were actually produced from the other accounting records maintained by the company. In other words the financial statements were not "made up" by the directors. If the accounting records are not consistent then the auditor will state this in the audit report.
P	**P**roper accounting records have been kept.	Statute law does state briefly what accounting records have to be kept by a company. If this was not the case then the auditor would say so in the audit report.
I	**I**nformation and explanations required by the auditor have been received.	The directors must provide the auditor with the information and explanations necessary to carry out his job. If the auditor does not obtain these then it will be stated in the audit report.
D	The **D**irectors' report is consistent with the financial statements.	The directors could try and give a different picture of the company in their report (especially if the company is losing money for example). If the auditor believes this has happened then the audit report will mention this fact.

3.8 Company internal regulation (audit committees)

Another "legal" bit that affects auditors in some countries is the audit committee. In some countries like the USA, the audit committee is a legal requirement; in others like the UK, audit committees are required as good practice by codes of governance. However, the function of the committee is almost the same, no matter why it is there.

Composition	Objective 1	Objective 2
2 to 3 non- executive directors, one having recent and relevant financial experience.	Liaise with the external auditors.	Provide additional credibility to the financial statements.
Why?	**Why?**	**Why?**
Non-executives ensure that the committee is unbiased regarding review of the financial statements and the member with experience provides the practical knowledge to undertake that review.	Provides the external auditors with a reporting mechanism separate from the board of directors – any concerns about the financial statements should be acted on.	Members of the company can see an additional level of review on the financial statements which should enhance their confidence in the directors and the accuracy of the financial statements.

The audit committee also provides an element of independence for the external auditor from the board of a company by:

• recommending which external auditor the board should appoint, and

• recommending the remuneration of the external auditor.

The audit committee will also monitor the independence of the external auditor to ensure there are no ethical threats which could result in a biased report. See chapter 2 for details on ethical threats.

3.9 An aside – auditing company systems – internal audit

The other regulatory matter to mention at this stage is internal audit.

 Internal audit basically provides an audit service to a company, but the auditors are employed by the company and work there full time.

The key features of internal and external audit are shown here

Feature	External Audit	Internal audit
Main objective	Audit and report on the financial statements	Acts as a management control – audits internal systems to ensure that those systems are working correctly.
Report to	The members	The audit committee initially and then the board of the company.
Required by	Statute	No legal requirement in many countries although compulsory in the USA and required by codes of governance in other countries such as the UK.
Type of work	Audit of financial statements	Can include, but not limited to, auditing of systems, audits on the economy and efficiency of operations, value for money audits, fraud investigations, advice on risk management etc.
Standard of work	Follow the ISAs	Will normally follow the ISAs as these represent best standard for audits – but are likely to carry out more testing than the ISA's would suggest as the type of the work is much more detailed.
Format of report	Prescribed by the ISAs	Can follow the ISAs but can also issue far more detailed reports where work carried out relates to other activities, as noted above.

However, the main reason for mentioning internal audit is that external auditors may rely on their work as part of a statutory audit. So here's the first bit of real ISA knowledge for you.

3.10 ISA 610 – Using the work of internal auditors

An external auditor may decide to use the work of internal auditors as part of the evidence for the external audit. Normally, this decreases the time (and therefore cost) of the audit.

Most auditing syllabuses contain a section on how external auditors rely on internal auditors. You need to learn how external auditors place reliance on internal auditors.

So, how does one group of auditors place reliance on another? There are three basic questions that the external auditor will need to ask which are given below, along with a summary of the ISA and an explanation of the ISA in clearer English.

Question	ISA summary	Which means
① Is the work of internal audit adequate for me to place reliance on? (ISA 610 para 9).	The external auditor will review the internal auditor's: • objectivity • technical competence • due professional care and ensure the internal auditor will communicate with the external auditor.	The external auditor is ensuring that the internal auditor follows the same ethical standards. You should recognise these from chapter 2.
② Is the work relevant to part of my external audit? (ISA 610 para 10).	The external auditor will ensure that the internal auditors' work covers some specific risk that the external auditor needs to audit.	As we will see later, the external auditor focuses specific audit work on "audit assertions" (see chapter 4). The internal auditors' work must be relevant to one of these assertions.
③ When I review the internal auditors' work, is it up to my standards? (ISA 610 para 12).	Internal audit work must be: • carried out by staff with sufficient training • properly supervised, reviewed and documented • have sufficient evidence to show how conclusions were reached • the final report is based on those conclusions • any problems found have been resolved.	Internal audit work must be at the same professional standard as external audit work. Basically that the ISAs have been followed and the conclusions reached are the same that the external auditor would reach if the same work was carried out.

So there we are. We will investigate the actual work of external auditors in the following chapters.

3.11 Summary of the summary

Finally the famous chapter summary (how many words this time? – see bottom of page).

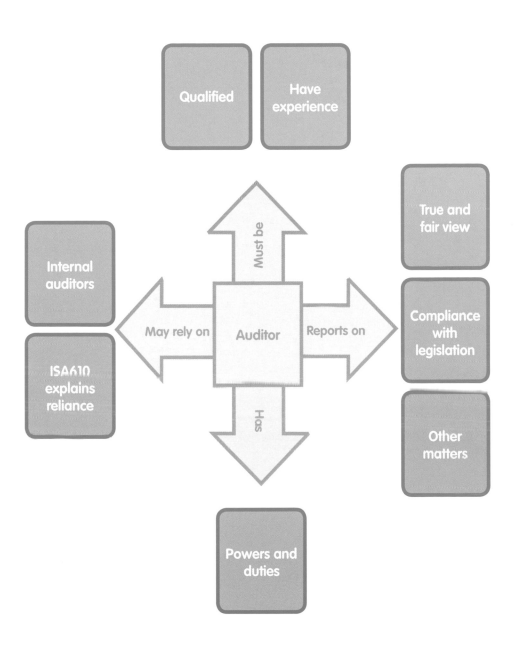

Chapter 4

The audit cycle

planning

4.1 Introduction – what will you learn?

We are now starting to work our way through an audit engagement. You will hopefully learn how to plan an audit, even though you may never have actually taken part in an audit.

I'll use a roadmap to guide us through this chapter. We start with an introduction to the standards that auditors must follow (the International Standards on Auditing) and then work through the planning process; that is all the things an auditor must do prior to actually collecting any audit evidence.

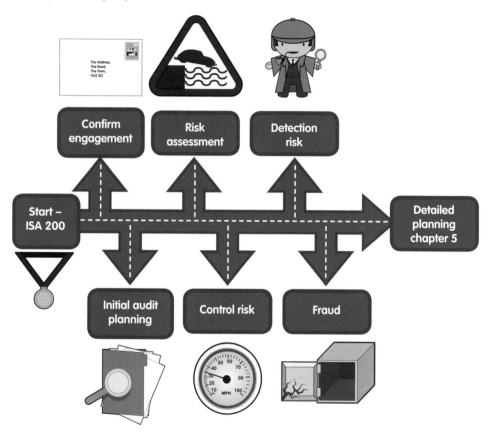

Event	Section reference
The start of the audit. This section introduces the purpose of ISAs and the key points of how an audit should be carried out. The key concept of audit risk is also introduced here as this forms the basis for a lot of audit planning.	4.3
Before an audit can start, the audit engagement must be confirmed with the client – the engagement letter forms the contract upon which audit work is based.	4.4
This is where audit planning really starts. In this section the overall audit plan is explained initially in terms of a strategy – or overall direction for the audit. Later, in chapter 5, the detail of an audit in terms of a plan for each part of the audit, will be explained.	4.5
Next there is some detailed risk assessment to try to ensure that nothing goes wrong during an audit (the road sign here being a hazard and not a reflection of an auditor's driving ability). Risk assessment starts with an overview of the company and the industry it is operating in.	4.6
Risk assessment then continues with control risk – that is how good the company's internal control systems are at preventing or detecting misstatements.	4.7
Risk assessment concludes with detection risk – an explanation of how the auditor uses risk to determine the amount of audit testing that is required at a client.	4.8
Finally in this chapter we look at the effect of fraud on the auditor. There is a separate ISA on fraud and this section summarises the detail from that ISA.	4.9

4.2 So, what is in this chapter?

This chapter walks you through the beginning of an audit. The aim is that you will understand in theory what happens on an audit even though you may never actually take part in an audit itself.

Audit planning is actually split into two sections in this book. This chapter explains the "big picture" of planning – that is how the auditor determines the overall audit strategy and makes an initial assessment of the audit work required. Chapter 5 then explains how an audit plan is developed for the detailed audit testing of each area of the financial statements (such as sales, purchases etc.).

4.3 Introduction to auditing

You will recall (hopefully) from chapter 2 that audits are conducted in accordance with International Standards on Auditing (or ISAs). There are relevant ISAs for most parts of an audit. There is also one ISA that explains the use of ISAs – this is ISA 200 *Overall objectives of the independent auditor and the conduct of an audit in accordance with international standards on auditing*, which is a long name for a small ISA so I'll just refer to it as ISA200.

Overview of the ISA

The ISA explains that an auditor needs to obtain sufficient appropriate audit evidence to form an opinion on the financial statements of an entity. This is the "gold standard" of the auditor (hence the medal!).

This means that the auditor must be fairly sure that financial statements are free from material misstatement (noting that misstatements can be caused by either fraud or error).

The ISA also notes that the auditor will apply the concept of materiality to audit work; more important parts of the financial statements or larger errors are more important to investigate (see chapter 5 for an explanation of materiality).

Finally, the ISA also states that all ISAs contain objectives and that the auditor must meet those objectives in every audit. If the objectives are not met then the auditor may need to amend the opinion on the financial statements or even resign. In other words, the auditor is very ethical (see chapter 2); where significant problems are found then resignation may be the only option – and this is more important than obtaining a fee.

As the ISA objectives are so important, they are included in this book. However, as objectives are frequently written in "auditor-speak", I've included a "translation" so you can hopefully understand what they mean. You will find this sort of table every time a new ISA is introduced; the ISA objective on the left and the plain English translation on the right.

d ISA Statement	Plain English statement
ISA detail here	ISA explanation here

I'll also include with each ISA a list of the key points you must understand from each ISA which can be used as a memory aid or simply a guide as to the contents of each section where ISAs are discussed.

With reference to ISA200, the things you must understand are:

1. how to audit using ISAs, and

2. how ISA200 explains audit risk and the overall approach to the audit.

These things are explained in the next sections.

Auditor's objectives

The main objective of the auditor is to ensure that the audit is completed in accordance with the specific requirements of the ISAs.

In this respect, the specific objectives that the auditor needs to attain as stated within ISA200 are:

🔲 ISA Statement	Plain English statement
In conducting an audit of financial statements, the overall objectives of the auditor are:	The auditor must:
(a) to obtain reasonable assurance about whether the financial statements as a whole are free from material misstatement, whether due to fraud or error, thereby enabling the auditor to express an opinion on whether the financial statements are prepared, in all material respects, in accordance with an applicable financial reporting framework, and	(a) collect audit evidence (and enough evidence) to be able to form an opinion on whether the financial statements are free from relatively large errors (that is material misstatements) and that the statements are prepared using the correct accounting regulations (that is the application of a financial reporting framework)
(b) to report on the financial statements, and communicate as required by the ISAs, in accordance with the auditor's findings.	(b) to tell the users of the financial statements what that opinion is.
In all cases when reasonable assurance cannot be obtained and a qualified opinion in the auditor's report is insufficient in the circumstances for purposes of reporting to the intended users of the financial statements, the ISAs require that the auditor disclaim an opinion or withdraw (or resign) from the engagement, where withdrawal is possible under applicable law or regulation.	Where the auditor cannot obtain sufficient evidence to determine whether or not the financial statements contain misstatements, and this problem is very significant, then the auditor must either state that the financial statements may not be correct or resign from the audit.

In other words, the auditor must collect the evidence required and if this is not possible then a qualification will normally occur. See chapter 9 for more details on audit qualifications.

What does ISA200 say about the conduct of an audit?

I've summarised ISA200 as a series of questions and answers between an auditor who is new to ISA200 and an expert on auditing, partly to maintain interest and partly because this is a succinct method of presenting this important information.

Auditor's question	Expert's answer
Do I need to comply with ethical requirements?	Of course, you are a member of a professional institute, what else did you expect?
Can I simply trust the company's management and information given to me?	Not a hope. You must plan your audit with professional scepticism – that is, only accept evidence and explanations where they appear reasonable; you must really have an expectation that material misstatements are likely and that you will find them. If you want a motto, then it's "Trust no one".
So I audit by rote then, simply following the rules?	Actually, no. Many situations in an audit require the application of judgement – this is what you qualified to do and why you are paid so much (!).
What is sufficient evidence?	Enough to conclude that the financial statements are free of material misstatement.
Must I comply with all ISAs?	Normally yes - and don't even think about not complying but stating in the audit report that you have complied; that is also against the ISA rules.
How do I know which bit of the ISA is important?	All ISAs have objectives – and you must comply with those objectives. Also in the ISAs, the word "**Shall**" is used to identify something that the auditor must do.
What happens if I think an ISA is not relevant?	Then you perform the audit procedures you think are needed – but I'd be prepared to justify that non-compliance to your professional institute when asked.
What happens if I cannot achieve an ISA objective?	Then you must consider modifying the audit opinion, as explained in the 700 series ISAs (and chapter 9 of this book).
Thank you for your help	You're welcome – that will be $500 for my time and expenses...!

So the moral of the story is – fix the expert's fee before work is carried out.

ISA200 and audit risk

ISA200 introduces the point that audits are risky for two reasons:

1. there is always the risk that financial statements contain material misstatements, and

2. there is the risk that the auditor may not detect those misstatements when collecting audit evidence.

In other words the overall risk is that the auditor may give an incorrect opinion at the end of the audit. This risk is called *audit risk*. Here is a diagram showing audit risk being the result of material misstatement and the auditor not detecting a misstatement:

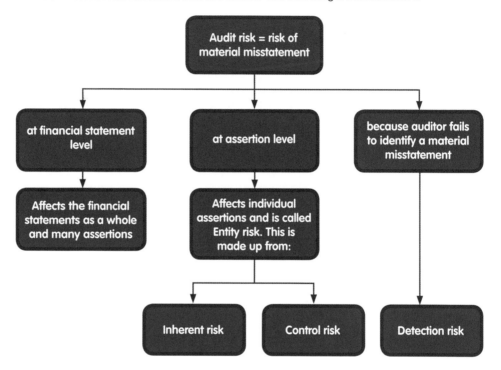

In other words, audit risk can affect the whole financial statements. This is unlikely, but we have already seen that if the auditor cannot obtain sufficient evidence then the audit report will be what is a called a disclaimer (the very bad report) or the auditor will resign.

For most situations the lack of evidence affects only one item on the financial statements; for example the auditor may not be sure that sales income is complete. In this case the audit report will still be qualified, but with a different and less serious opinion (see chapter 9 for more detail).

The reference to *individual assertions* relates to specific audit objectives. These are explained in more detail in chapters 6 and 7. For now, just think of the auditor being uncertain about say the completeness of income, as mentioned above.

Finally, you can see from the diagram that audit risk is actually made up from three elements; two relating to the entity and one to audit testing. In more detail these risks are:

Risk	d Definition from ISA200	Plain English explanation
Inherent	The susceptibility of an assertion about a class of transaction, account balance or disclosure to a misstatement that could be material, either individually or when aggregated with other misstatements, before consideration of any related controls.	There is the possibility of a material misstatement in the financial statements as a result of factors inherent in the situation of that client. For example, in a company dealing primarily with cash, completeness of income may be difficult to determine because cash is easy to steal.
Control	The risk that a misstatement that could occur in an assertion about a class of transaction, account balance or disclosure and that could be material, either individually or when aggregated with other misstatements, will not be prevented, or detected and corrected, on a timely basis by the entity's internal control.	There is also the risk of misstatement because the company's internal control systems do not prevent or detect an error. For example, in a shop using cash, completeness of income could be confirmed by agreeing the amount that should be in a cash till to the actual cash in that till (the till itself keeping a record of the cash sales). However there will still be a weakness; the control assumes that the person operating the till records the cash sale. No recording of sale means that some cash is not included in the total and this could therefore still be stolen.
Detection	The risk that the procedures performed by the auditor to reduce audit risk to an acceptably low level will not detect a misstatement that exists and that could be material, either individually or when aggregated with other misstatements.	Finally, there is the risk that the auditor's procedures do not detect a misstatement. In other words the auditor either does not plan audit procedures correctly or there is a weakness in the audit procedures actually used. For example, to test completeness of income as noted above, the auditor needs to observe the person using the till to ensure all income is recorded So failure to do this test will increase detection risk.

The only risk that the auditor can control is detection risk. The entity risks of inherent risk and control risk are determined by the type of client (inherent risk) and the client's approach to controls.

Example of inherent risk and control risk

To make these risks clearer, imagine the situation where you want to cross a road. There is the inherent risk that you may be injured crossing the road because you are hit by a car. This risk is inherent in the need to cross the road – roads have cars on them and so there is a risk of being hit.

However, you can mitigate this risk by crossing the road carefully; for example by using a pedestrian crossing (a place where traffic lights stop cars so people can cross the road). This control system should therefore be used to decrease the risk of being injured crossing the road.

Company systems are in many ways no different to this situation. There are risks and the company establishes controls to ensure that those risks are minimised.

I do need to explain audit risk (and its individual risk elements) in more detail. However, before doing this, we need to start the audit. The next section therefore explains the process of appointing the auditor (that is engagement letters) and then subsequent sections move onto risk assessment – this is where audit risk will appear again.

4.4 Engagement letters

Before an audit can start, there has to be a contract between the client company and the auditor to appoint the auditor and confirm exactly what work will be carried out. This contract is the engagement letter with the relevant ISA being 210 *Agreeing the terms of audit engagements*.

Overview of the ISA

The ISA confirms that an engagement letter should be obtained prior to audit work commencing. The letter will normally be reviewed and signed by the auditor and management each year, although this not strictly necessary. Significant changes such as new management at the client will mean that the letter is re-sent to remind management of their responsibilities.

Key things you must understand are:

1. the checks the auditor makes prior to accepting the audit engagement

2. the standard contents of the engagement letter, and

3. problems that can occur after the engagement letter has been signed.

These things are explained in the next sections.

Auditor's objectives

The main objectives of the auditor are to ensure that the management of the company understand the need for an audit.

The specific objectives that the auditor must achieve are:

d ISA Statement	Plain English statement
The objective of the auditor is to accept or continue an audit engagement only when the basis upon which it is to be performed has been agreed, through (a) establishing whether the preconditions for an audit are present; and	An auditor only accepts an audit engagement where initially the management of a company are using an appropriate financial reporting framework – this is actually what the "precondition" in the ISA statement refers to.
(b) confirming that there is a common understanding between the auditor and management and, where appropriate, those charged with governance of the terms of the audit engagement.	An auditor also ensures that management do understand the purpose of an audit.

Checks prior to signing the engagement letter

Before the auditor accepts an engagement, there are two key questions that must be answered relating to the financial reporting framework and management's responsibilities in addition to ethical considerations already covered previously. These are shown below.

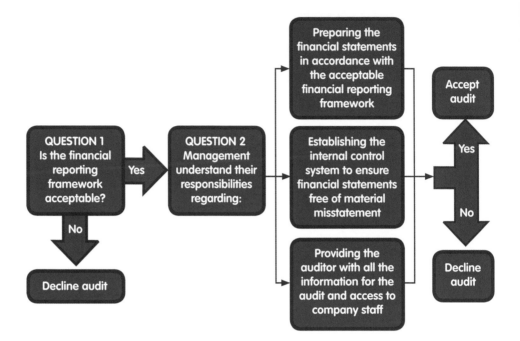

Regarding the two questions:

*   The financial reporting framework refers to the use of IFRS's or similar recognised standards. Financial statements should now be prepared to comply with recognised standards.

*   Management responsibilities refer to things that management must do; the auditor ensures management understand these things.

If the auditor can accept the audit, then the engagement letter can be written and sent to management for approval.

Typical contents of engagement letter

An engagement letter is normally several pages in length and contains several standard "sections". The main sections are given below, although the ISA does mention (in paragraphs A23 to A25) other points that can be included.

☾ Engagement letter section	Why is it there?
Objective and scope of the audit of financial statements.	To confirm that the auditor is carrying out an audit under appropriate legislation and that the ISAs are used as the basis of the audit work.
Responsibilities of the auditor.	To confirm that the auditor is responsible for the audit; not for financial statement preparation or to detect all fraud and/or error.
Responsibilities of management.	To confirm that management are responsible for the preparation of the financial statements and to ensure that those statements are free from material misstatement.
Identification of the applicable financial reporting framework for the preparation of the financial statements.	So management and the auditor know what this framework is (for example use of IFRS).
State the expected form and content of the auditor's report.	To confirm that the report is based on the ISA's.
Basis of fees.	To provide information to management that the fees are calculated on time spent and grade of staff used.
Management representations.	A note to management that representations will be required at the end of the audit (see chapter 8 for more details on management representations).
Request to management to confirm receipt of the letter.	The confirmation effectively completes the contract between the auditor and management.

When the auditor receives the engagement letter, countersigned by management, then the audit can commence.

Problems after signing the engagement letter

Very occasionally, management may try and change the scope of the auditor's work after the engagement letter has been signed. Examples of changes include:

- change in the level of assurance – the company may no longer require a statutory audit but simply a "review" of the financial statements

- the need to meet new country specific legal requirements.

If the auditor agrees with the changes, then a new engagement letter will be signed. However, if the changes are not satisfactory then the auditor will have to consider withdrawing from the audit. For example, if management inform the auditor that they will no longer provide the auditor with all the information required, the auditor cannot complete the audit and so stopping the audit may be the only viable option.

4.5 Planning the audit – the start

Having agreed to do an audit, the auditor can now start planning – or setting out the "map" for the audit. ISA 300 *Planning the audit of financial statements* is useful here.

Overview of the ISA

The ISA sets out, fairly succinctly, the reasons for planning an audit and provides an overview of the activities that the auditor will carry out. More detailed planning is deferred to another ISA (315) which we will look at later in this chapter.

Key things you must understand are:

1. what audit planning is

2. the benefits of planning, and

3. the main sections of an audit strategy.

These things are explained in the next sections.

Auditor's objectives

Planning an audit is like a car journey; there is no point getting into your car and driving unless you know where you are going; you need a map (OK, or a satellite navigation system). The plan is therefore to create the map for the audit.

There is only one objective in this ISA:

d ISA Statement	Plain English statement
The objective of the auditor is to plan the audit so that it will be performed in an effective manner.	The auditor needs to plan an audit so that the audit is successful – that is an appropriate audit opinion is reached. The plan helps the auditor reach that opinion by giving the framework for the audit.

Benefits of audit planning:

In other words, the ISA does state an audit must be planned. You may ask why bother? Again the ISA provides an answer with a list of benefits of planning. Here's the list with the normal plain English section and a link to the audit of 27/4Books.

ISA statement	Plain English	ⓧ Example from 27/4Books
Helping the auditor to devote appropriate attention to important areas of the audit.	Decreases the risk of missing material errors.	Inventory is quite large; attend inventory count and audit inventory systems.
Helping the auditor identify and resolve potential problems on a timely basis.	To ensure that problems do not become serious.	Not sure what the problems are yet – but better to find out about them than ignore.
Helping the auditor properly organise and manage the audit engagement so that it is performed in an effective and efficient manner.	Resources such as audit staff used to maximum benefit – staff are not sitting around waiting for work.	Only book staff for the audit when confirmed with client when the financial statements will be ready for audit.
Assisting in the selection of engagement team members with appropriate levels of capabilities and competence to respond to anticipated risks, and the proper assignment of work to them.	Ensure the audit team members have appropriate skills and experience for the client being audited.	27/4Books systems are mainly computerised – need to ensure computer audit specialists are on audit team so systems can be audited correctly.
Facilitating the direction and supervision of engagement team members and the review of their work.	The audit team are monitored and Manager / Partner reviews booked in advance to ensure work carried out correctly.	Work on difficult audit areas (such as computer systems) reviewed by manager relatively early in the audit to ensure there are no major problems.
Assisting, where applicable, in coordination of work done by auditors of components and experts.	Booking specialist staff for assistance with the audit of subsidiaries ("components" in ISA speak) or valuation of specialist items.	A professional valuer may be used to provide a market valuation on 27/4Books property such as the warehouse.

Not an easy list to remember. However, this may help – the 6 *italic* words refer to the 6 main benefits of planning.

 Attention to *Problems Manages* the *Team* with *Supervision* which is *Expert.*

Elements of the audit strategy

Planning at the beginning of the audit also means setting out the audit strategy – this is the "big picture" or guide to the audit. The strategy shows in overview three things, being the:

1. audit scope : what needs to be audited

2. audit timing : when the audit will take place

3. audit direction : the general approach to the audit in terms of testing methods (more on these later).

The aim of the strategy is to guide the development of the audit plan. Remember if the audit strategy is correct there will still be time to dance – there is a life outside of audit.

Did you miss that? Strategy correct so **S**till **T**ime to **D**ance – three main things that the strategy does.

The three elements of strategy have a few general actions associated with them – as shown in the following diagram.

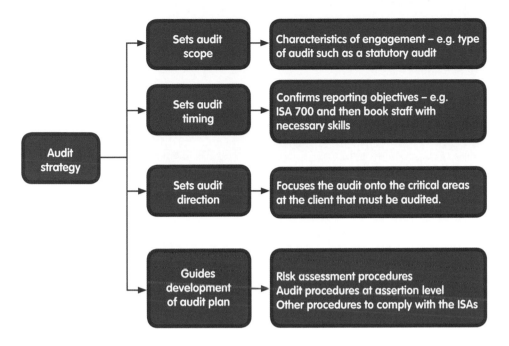

As you can see, strategy also means guiding the audit plan - this is the detailed approach to the audit of the different account balances such as sales or receivables. There is more detail on setting strategy in the following sections.

4.6 Planning the audit – risk assessment

With overall planning complete, the auditor can start on planning the audit in detail. ISA 315 *Identifying and assessing the risks of material misstatement through understanding the entity and its environment* is the relevant ISA here.

Overview of the ISA

This ISA follows on from ISA300 (already explained in section 4.5) to explain some of the detailed planning that the auditor must carry out on any audit.

Key things you must understand are:

1. what risk assessment procedures are, and

2. how risk assessment procedures can be applied to an audit.

These things are explained in the next sections.

Auditor's objectives

The overall objective of the auditor is to try to ensure that the financial statements are free of material misstatement.

Here is the objective stated in this ISA:

d ISA Statement	Plain English statement
The objective of the auditor is to identify and assess the risks of material misstatement, whether due to fraud or error, at the financial statement and assertion levels, through understanding the entity and its environment, including the entity's internal control, thereby providing a basis for designing and implementing responses to the assessed risks of material misstatement.	The auditor must try to identify where material misstatements will occur and then design audit procedures to try to ensure that material misstatements have not occurred. The reference to financial statements and assertions means the auditor is concerned not only with the financial statements as a whole, but also the accuracy of individual balances in those financial statements.

Risk assessment procedures - overview

One of the main reasons that the auditor is carrying out this risk assessment is to try to identify whether there is the possibility of material misstatements in the accounts of the company. In terms of audit risk, the auditor is assessing inherent risk (as mentioned in section 4.3, remember?) and then control risk; inherent risk relating to the industry and business of the client and control risk to how good the control system actually is.

The risk assessment procedures in ISA315 can be summarised as shown below. There are four stages to assessing risk; these are noted on the diagram and explained in the table after the diagram.

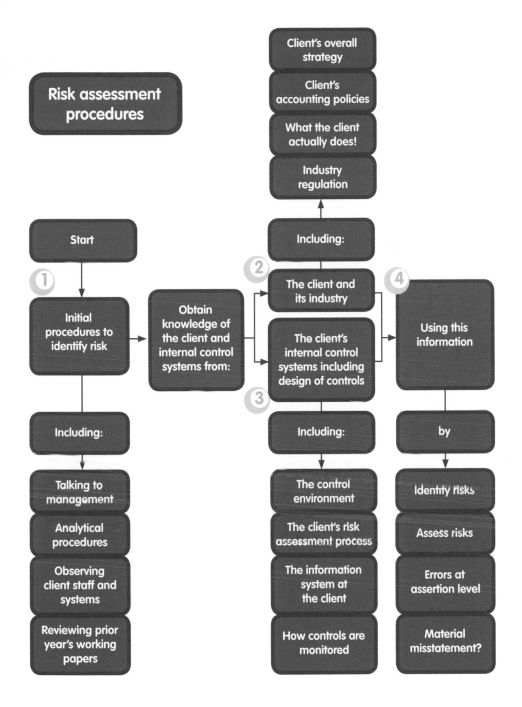

Risk assessment procedures

Start

① Initial procedures to identify risk

Obtain knowledge of the client and internal control systems from:

② The client and its industry

③ The client's internal control systems including design of controls

④ Using this information

Including:

Client's overall strategy

Client's accounting policies

What the client actually does!

Industry regulation

Including:

Talking to management

Analytical procedures

Observing client staff and systems

Reviewing prior year's working papers

Including:

The control environment

The client's risk assessment process

The information system at the client

How controls are monitored

by

Identify risks

Assess risks

Errors at assertion level

Material misstatement?

Explanation of risk assessment procedures

Stage	Explanation	Key activities – further information
①	The auditor starts to obtain detailed information about the client. These initial risk assessment procedures provide further background to the client company, but are not sufficient by themselves to identify risks – more detailed work is needed in stages 2 and 3 below. After the evidence has been collected, all the members of the audit team meet to identify and discuss risks which may affect the client company. In other words, risk assessment is meant to be a group activity rather than relying solely on the knowledge of any one person.	Talking to management as they have (or should have) detailed knowledge of the company. Performing analytical procedures (see chapter 5 for more detail). Observing client staff working, to ensure controls are being used correctly. Using information from other sources such as other work carried out for the client company.
②	Risk assessment continues by finding out more about the client company. This means obtaining information about the company and its activities from various sources. Some of these risks will be inherent in the client – that is they cannot be affected by the auditor. The auditor is again expanding the amount of evidence to find risks that could affect the client.	**Industry regulation** – relates to additional rules for that industry e.g. compliance with health and safety requirements. **Client's business** – there will be risks relating to what the client does; for example a company dealing with cash sales has a higher risk of cash being stolen. **Accounting policies** – should be appropriate (this will be ascertained prior to accepting the audit). **Client's overall strategy** – some strategies will involve more risk, such as in recent years banks lending long term and borrowing short term.

Stage	Explanation	Key activities – further information
③	The third part of obtaining information about the client relates to the company's own internal systems and processes. Here the auditor is ensuring that the control environment is satisfactory – that is the company's internal control systems are sufficient to identify and correct any misstatements. The auditor also needs to ensure that the control system is checked by management to prove it is working correctly. In many cases this involves checking the work carried out by the internal audit function.	**Control environment** – ensuring management recognise the need for good internal controls (see section 4.7 for more detail). **Risk assessment process** – ensuring that management do have some method for identifying risks and then taking action to mitigate those risks. **Information systems** – are sufficient to provide management with information to identify possible risks. **Monitoring of controls** – that controls are actually checked to make sure they are working – this is a job for Internal Audit (see chapter 5).
④	Finally, all this information will be collated together and the auditor will try and determine whether misstatement can occur either: 1. in the financial statements as a whole, or 2. regarding one or more assertions affecting individual balances in the financial statements.	The process is: 1. identify the risk 2. assess the risk 3. determine whether misstatement could occur for any assertion 4. determine whether those misstatements can be material.

Risks in stage ② may also be termed inherent risks – that is those risks relating to the business or industry that the client is working in. Where auditing questions refer to business risks they normally mean inherent risks; things that the auditor cannot change but their company is affected by.

Risk identification, assertions and 27/4Books

As mentioned at the beginning of this chapter, the ISA keeps referring to "*Assertions*". These are things that the auditor is trying to prove regarding the financial statements; they are explained in more detail in chapters 6 and 7. Briefly for now, the management will assert something about the financial statements, for example that sales are completely recorded. The auditor will then obtain evidence to try and identify whether or not this assertion is correct; or risks that the assertion cannot be true.

In relation to 27/4Books this could mean:

Stage	Example audit procedure	Possible situation
①	Discussion with 27/4Books management about the company trading over the year and possibly draft financial statements.	Management inform the auditor that 27/4Books has expanded and now has a subsidiary in another country.
②	Management confirm that 27/4Books strategy is to expand and that the subsidiary will be accounted for using standard accounting practice.	The auditor reviews the financial statements of 27/4Books confirming accounting treatment of the subsidiary and determining the size of the investment.
③	Discussion with management shows that controls are still being tested in the main business of 27/4Books by their internal audit department, although controls in the new subsidiary have yet to be determined.	The auditor will attempt to obtain information about the new subsidiary and the systems and controls there. This may mean asking management to obtain more information. However, lack of information is concerning as misstatements could occur from lack of controls.

Stage	Example audit procedure	Possible situation
④	The auditor concludes that misstatements could occur in the subsidiary as there is insufficient information to confirm controls are effective.	The auditor has therefore: Identified the risk that controls may be poor in the subsidiary. Assessed the risk as far as possible noting the need for additional information. Determined whether misstatements could occur for any assertion – for example sales may not be complete due to lack of controls. Determined whether those misstatements can be material – due to lack of information this assessment is not complete; more information will have to be collected using more audit procedures.

 Other inherent risks that could affect 27/4Books include:

- Inventory being stolen. 27/4Books is a book wholesaler; it owns a warehouse which contains the book inventory. It could be quite easy for an employee to steal a book they want to read.
- General demand for books. If people decide that they want to read fewer books, or move to other book formats such as e-books, then this will decrease demand for books and therefore sales for 27/4Books.

These are risks that 27/4Books is automatically subject to. The risks may be mitigated using controls, as shown below, but overall the risks cannot be avoided as they are part of selling books.

4.7 Control risk and Internal control elements

Overview of an internal control system

 Section 4.3 introduced the concept of control risk – that is the risk that misstatements in a set of accounts would not be prevented or detected by the company's internal control system. However, I omitted to explain what an internal control system actually is. It's now time to remedy that omission.

An internal control system is established in a company to try to prevent misstatements occurring or where this is not possible, to detect that a misstatement has occurred.

ISA315 provides an explanation of the "components" or the things that go to make up an internal control system in a company. I've summarised these below – if you want more detail then please have a look at Appendix 1 of ISA315.

Internal control component	Explanation
Control environment.	This is the overall approach to controls within a company. Basically it means that all the employees in a company, from senior management to the most junior staff are aware of the need for controls. Also, there are control systems established and all staff do follow those controls; it is seen as an ethical duty to do this.
Entity's risk assessment process.	Management have methods of identifying risks; with those risks occurring both within and external to the company.
Information systems including the related business processes relevant to financial reporting and communication.	The company's information systems (normally computerised) are sufficient to record all the transactions of the company completely and accurately.
Control activities.	These are the detailed controls within a company which try to ensure misstatements do not occur. There are four main categories of controls which are explained below.
Monitoring of controls.	Management must monitor controls to make sure that they are effective. This task is normally delegated to the internal audit department. See chapter 5.13 for more information on internal audit.

Potentially the most important internal control component, at least from the auditor's point-of-view, is control activities. As we will see in chapter 5, these are the detailed controls that the auditor will test to ensure that company systems are working correctly.

Control activities

These will be mentioned in chapter 5 as the basis for an auditor developing what is termed "tests of controls" – that is audit procedures to ensure that controls are actually working. Chapters 6 and 7 then provide examples of those controls for different transactions and balances within 27/4Books.

For now, here is the list of control activities, along with an explanation of the control and an example from 27/4Books.

Control activity	Explanation	Example from 27/4Books audit
Performance reviews	Activities such as reviewing current performance against budgets and prior periods and then taking action to investigate unusual items and correct errors.	Comparing the 20X1 financial information with 20X0, identifying unusual changes and finding reasons for those changes. This is a type of analytical review – see chapter 5.
Information processing (1) **Application controls**	These are controls which apply to the processing within individual applications (such as sales or purchases) within a company. They include: 1. checking the arithmetical accuracy of records 2. maintaining and reviewing control accounts and trial balances 3. automated controls such as edit checks of input data and numerical sequence checks, and 4. manual follow-up of exception reports.	Examples within 27/4Books relevant to the four controls are: 1. adding up the sales day book to ensure that the total is correct 2. ensuring that the receivables ledger control account agrees to the individual balances making up that account 3. computer controls on input such as ensuring that customer account numbers are valid, and 4. management investigating reports on missing documents such as despatch notes which do not appear to have an invoice associated with them.

⚷ Control activity	Explanation	ℯ Example from 27/4Books audit
Information processing (2) **General IT controls**	These are controls which specifically apply to the computerised systems within a company. They include: 1. program change controls 2. controls that restrict access to programs or data 3. controls over the implementation of new releases of packaged software applications, and 4. controls over system software.	Examples within 27/4Books relevant to the four controls are (although note these controls are likely to be the same in most companies): 1. changes to programs requiring authorisation from specific officials in the company 2. passwords barring most staff from accessing computer programs 3. again senior officials authorise use of new software releases 4. the computer system generates a list of all amendments to computer software.
Physical controls	These are controls to ensure that the assets of the company are not stolen and include: 1. the physical security of assets 2. the authorisation for access to computer programs and data files, and 3. the periodic counting and comparison with amounts shown on control records.	Examples of each of these controls: 1. locking the book warehouse at the end of each day 2. passwords to access different parts of the computer program 3. performing an inventory count to agree books in the warehouse to the computerised inventory systems.

Control activity	Explanation	Example from 27/4Books audit
Segregation of duties	Each transaction has different people to: 1. authorise 2. record, and 3. maintain custody of any assets relating to that transaction. This means that to create fraudulent transactions there needs to be collusion.	For example, to purchase books, there are different people to: 1. authorise the purchase of the books 2. record the physical receipt of books into 27/4's warehouse, and 3. maintain security in the warehouse including removing those books ordered by customers. If one person could purchase and receive the books they could order books they wanted and steal them as received rather than place those books in the warehouse.
Other control activities	The ISA notes that there may be other control activities such as authorisation controls for some transactions with those controls varying depending on the nature of the transaction.	The board of 27/4Books would need to authorise the purchase of a new subsidiary but a purchasing manager would have the authority to order more books for re-sale.

Examples of many of these controls, particularly the application controls, can be found in chapters 6 and 7 where detailed audit work on 27/4Books financial statements is discussed.

Remember that authorisation is just an example of other controls that can be used. The five main controls in the ISA can still be remembered as PAG post-script (or PAGPS as the first letters. Performance review, Application controls, General IT controls, Physical controls, Segregation of duties).

From the examination point-of-view, this is a critical list to learn; many examination questions focus on requiring the candidate to identify control activities in a scenario.

4.8 Detection risk and the audit risk model

Detection risk : more detail

 As noted in section 4.3, detection risk is the risk that audit procedures fail to detect a misstatement. In other words on an audit, the auditor identifies an area where misstatement can occur, has planned audit procedures to try and ensure that there is no misstatement, but unfortunately those procedures do not work so the auditor may still be unclear as to whether there is a misstatement or not.

There are two main reasons why audit procedures may "fail":

Reason audit procedure "fails"	Explanation
Sampling risk 1. The sample chosen is not representative of the population.	The auditor does not have time to actually test or audit all the transactions in a company (imagine having to check all the sales invoices in 27/4Books back to the inventory records to ensure that goods were actually despatched for each sale – there would be thousands each year!). Rather, a small sample of items is chosen to test (see chapter 5 for more detail on statistical sampling and how to choose items for testing). The auditor assumes that the sample of items tested will show the same results as the whole population, if that was tested. If this is not the case then the audit conclusions will be wrong. The problem, of course, is that the auditor does not know if this problem has occurred because the whole population is not tested. Sampling risk is therefore minimised by the audit firm using some recognised method of selecting items for testing.

⚓ Reason audit procedure "fails"	Explanation
Non-sampling risk 2. The auditor has failed to apply audit procedures correctly, or interpreted the results of those procedures incorrectly.	Audit procedures can fail for many other reasons – these reasons are grouped together under the general heading of "non-sampling risk". Non-sampling risk can occur for reasons such as: 1. the auditor does not use the statistical sampling method correctly and chooses items for testing different from those prescribed by the method, or 2. the auditor interprets the results of procedures incorrectly. Non-sampling risk is minimised by ensuring that the auditor is trained correctly to use the sampling method and audit procedures.

 As an example, here's a procedure from 27/4Books with an example of sampling risk and non-sampling risk (the examples must be viewed independently; they do not relate to each other).

Procedure	Example of sampling risk	Example of non-sampling risk
Select a sample of despatch notes and ensure that a sales invoice has been raised for each despatch note.	The conclusion from testing is that all despatch notes have a sales invoice raised. However, if the whole population had been tested the auditor would have found due to a computer program error, despatches made on the 31st of the month were not invoiced; unfortunately the sample of despatch notes tested did not include any dated on the 31st.	The auditor found one despatch note where no invoice had been raised. However, this error was thought to be unimportant as the despatch note was for one book; the error was therefore ignored. As we will see in chapter 5, this is an incorrect conclusion; any error found during statistical sampling is important and must be investigated.

Detection risk is one of the factors used by the auditor to determine how many items will be included in an audit sample. The auditor gives a value to detection risk; this value then determines the confidence that the auditor needs that material misstatements have not occurred.

For example

- If detection risk was 5%, the auditor would need 95% confidence from audit procedures that there are no material misstatements.

- If detection risk was 45%, the auditor would need only 55% confidence from audit procedures that there are no material misstatements.

- If detection risk was 80%, the auditor would be satisfied with only 20% confidence from audit procedures.

In other words, the *higher* detection risk, the *lower* the amount of confidence needed concerning material misstatements and the *lower* the number of items to be tested. Yes I know this appears wrong – you must think of the audit confidence that the auditor wants to obtain – lower confidence levels are easier to obtain than higher, because this means less audit evidence needs to be collected.

Think of a pack of 52 cards; I want to make sure that the pack is a "real" pack of playing cards – that is it contains all four suits and the cards 1 to King in each suit. I can look at a few cards and as long as they are different; (have a selection of suits and numbers) I'm fairly sure (say 30% confident) that the pack does contain all the playing cards. However, if I want to be really sure (have 100% confidence) then I'll need to look at all the cards. Higher levels of confidence require more testing – OK?

Hopefully you got that? That is the worst bit of auditing, in terms of numbers, over with. We can now see how detection risk fits into the audit risk model.

Audit risk model

All this talk of risk now leads to what is generally known as the "Audit risk model".

Remember that this chapter is about audit planning and how the auditor approaches an audit engagement. We already know that the auditor considers and makes an evaluation of risk in two areas:

- inherent risk – risks arising from the industry that the client company is in, and

- control risk – risks arising from poorly designed or weak internal control systems.

That is Entity risk. We also know that the overall risk on an audit is called audit risk – this is the risk that the auditor forms an incorrect conclusion on the financial statements; for example, that the financial statements contain a material misstatement but audit procedures have failed to detect this misstatement.

Finally we know that audit risk is a function of inherent risk, control risk and detection risk.

So, in practice what an auditor does is give values to Audit risk, Inherent risk and Control risk – the audit firm's audit approach manual will help the auditor make this judgement. The values range between 0 – being no risk at all, and 1 being very high risk. Having allocated these values, the amount of detection risk – and therefore audit confidence required will be known. This in turn gives an indication of the amount of audit evidence that must be collected.

In general terms

- Audit risk will be set at 5% - that is the auditor needs to be 95% confident that the audit opinion is correct.

- Inherent risk will be set depending on the risk associated with the business – riskier companies have higher values of inherent risk.

- Control risk will be set according to the auditor's evaluation of the internal control system – poorer control systems (which mean higher possibility of missing errors) have higher values of control risk.

This means that detection risk will be determined by the auditor (or more precisely the auditor's audit procedures manual) based on these other judgements. Look at the following diagram:

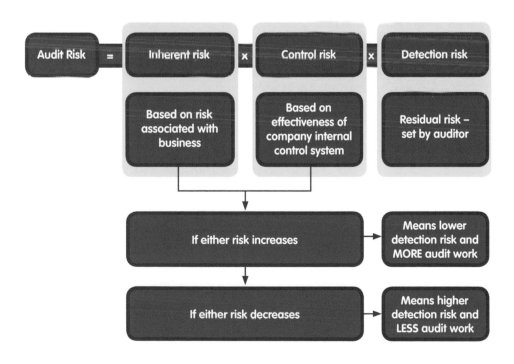

This is logical – check the examples:

Think about a company with really poor internal control systems. The auditor would give Control risk a high value – say 80% - which means that detection risk will need to be low to keep the overall value of audit risk of 5%. Low detection risk, we know, means more audit work – which is correct because the internal control systems are poor.

OR

Think about a company where inherent risk falls to be very low (perhaps a cash receipts system has been replaced with a credit card system minimising the possibility of cash fraud). As inherent risk falls so detection risk increases and the auditor does less work. This is correct because there is less risk now of fraud occurring.

In terms of 27/4Books the following assessment could be made:

Audit risk =	Inherent risk X	Control risk X	Detection risk
Set at 5%	Fairly stable industry (people like reading books)	Good control systems with few weaknesses	To meet audit risk requirement risk assessment set as HIGH
	Risk assessment LOW	Risk assessment LOW	

The high detection risk means low confidence required from audit procedures and therefore relatively few items need to be tested.

Summary

So there you have it – how auditors determine in general terms how much audit evidence to collect. The "mix" of evidence (and there are three main sources of evidence to choose from) will be discussed in chapter 5.

4.9 Fraud

Fraud relates to the possibility that the financial statements may be incorrect due to deception or potentially illegal activities. The auditor is therefore interested in fraud, not because this is an illegal activity, but because the financial statements may contain material misstatements.

Audit work regarding fraud is explained in ISA 240 *The auditors responsibilities relating to fraud in an audit of financial statements.*

Overview of the ISA

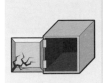 The ISA explains that there are two types of intentional misstatements that the auditor must be concerned about. These are:

1. misstatements resulting from fraudulent reporting, and

2. misstatements resulting from misappropriation of assets.

Fraudulent reporting relates to the financial statements containing inaccuracies to "hide" problems such as liabilities not being included in those financial statements. Misappropriation of assets relates to situations where assets have been stolen but those assets are still shown on the statement of financial position as being assets of the company.

Remember though that the auditor is not primarily responsible for preventing or detecting fraud, this is the job of management. To repeat, the auditor is only concerned about fraud because the financial statements may contain a material misstatement.

Key things you must understand are:

1. what fraud is in the context of auditing, and

2. audit work required in respect of fraud.

These things are explained in the next sections.

Auditor's objectives

The auditor needs to ensure that the financial statements are free from material misstatement; this includes misstatement where management may be attempting to deceive the auditor.

The specific objectives from the ISA are as follows:

d ISA Statement	Plain English statement
To identify and assess the risks of material misstatement of the financial statements due to fraud.	The auditor needs to find out whether fraud could occur at the client and if so how serious the fraud could be.
To obtain sufficient appropriate audit evidence regarding the assessed risks of material misstatement due to fraud, through designing and implementing appropriate responses.	Depending on the risk of fraud occurring, the auditor needs to obtain audit evidence to make a judgement on whether there are material misstatements due to fraud. Where the risk of fraud is higher, then more audit evidence will be required to make this judgement.
To respond appropriately to fraud or suspected fraud identified during the audit.	Where fraud or suspected fraud is found during the audit, the auditor must decide what to do; possibilities include reporting to management through to qualifying the audit report.

What is fraud?

Fraud is an intentional act by one or more individuals among management, those charged with governance, employees, or third parties, involving the use of deception to obtain an unjust or illegal advantage. In other words, any person within a company could attempt to commit fraud so the auditor must always be "looking out" for fraud at all times during the audit.

The auditor will be concerned about fraud because if fraud has occurred, the financial statements may include material misstatements. This means that the auditor is not actually making a determination whether fraud has taken place – as in the act being illegal. The auditor is simply concerned that the financial statements are correct; it will be up to management or any external authorities such as the police to actually say whether any irregularities found are actually "fraudulent".

Audit work regarding fraud

ISA 240 contains a lot of advice to an auditor on how to conduct an audit considering the possibility of fraud. I've summarised this work under five main headings below:

1	2	3	4	5
Commence audit with professional scepticism	Find out how management assess and address the risk of fraud	Assess the risk of material misstatement due to fraud and take action to limit that risk	Evaluate the audit evidence obtained including management representations	Communicate any problems to those charged with governance

Stage	Explanation
1	The auditor starts the audit as always (see ISA 200 in section 4.3 above) with an attitude of professional scepticism. This means that the auditor will not trust management and not believe that accounting records are genuine unless evidence is obtained to suggest this is the case. The whole audit team will be involved in "looking out for" fraud.
2	Before the auditor collects any audit evidence, the main emphasis on audit work regarding fraud is to find out how management evaluate the risk of fraud. The auditor will also want to know what procedures are put in place by management to prevent and detect fraud. Where the internal control system appears satisfactory (see Control Risk section 4.7 above) then the auditor gains some confidence that fraud has not taken place.
3	At a more detailed level, the auditor looks for specific situations where fraud could occur e.g. cash being stolen. Specific controls to prevent these frauds will be reviewed to ensure that they are effective. One specific concern here is what is known as *management override*. This is the possibility that senior management simply ignore the internal control system and make accounting entries for their own benefit. The auditor will need to determine whether management have taken this action, by talking to management and reviewing unusual transactions such as journal entries.
4	Towards the end of the audit, the auditor reviews all the evidence obtained and tries to decide whether or not fraud has occurred. Where significant fraud is suspected the auditor may even need to consider resigning because sufficient audit evidence to form an opinion will not be available (see chapter 9 on audit qualifications). The auditor will always obtain a management representation letter point (see chapter 8 for more detail on this letter) to confirm management's responsibilities regarding fraud.
5	Finally the auditor will report any suspected fraud as follows: • To any relevant authorities – in some countries the auditor has to report suspicions of fraud – for example in the European Union under Anti-Money Laundering regulations • To those charged with governance – that is the management and board of their client in a formal letter, and • Where fraud means that the financial statements contain a material misstatement, by qualifying the audit report to bring this matter to the attention of the members.

And that's fraud – in an audit context.

4.10 So where are we now?

Part way through planning an audit. We know what the overall audit strategy is, but have yet to determine the approach to individual sections of the financial statements. Chapter 5 continues audit planning by looking in detail at how sales, purchases and other account balances are actually audited.

4.11 Summary of the summary

Finally the end of chapter summary – a bit longer now than others:

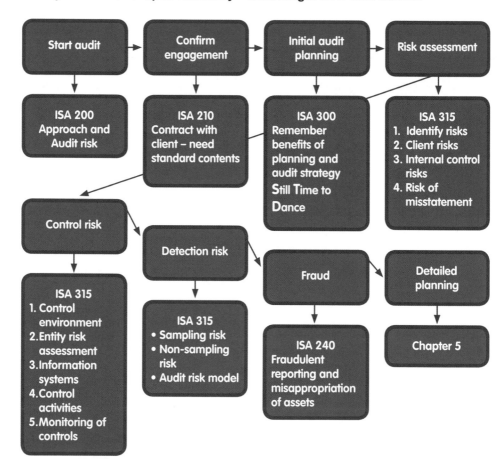

Chapter 5

The audit cycle
detailed planning

A student's guide to Auditing By Alan Lewin

5.1 Introduction – what will you learn?

Having set the audit strategy in the last chapter, this chapter explains all the different activities that must be carried out up to and including collecting audit evidence. This is a lot of ground to cover, as the road map below suggests. So hang on, this is going to be a long ride, but hopefully we'll get to the end in one piece.

Here's the roadmap for this chapter with an overview for each section.

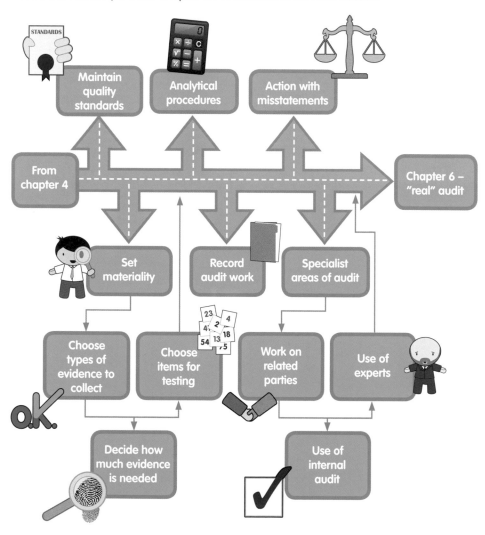

In overview, these diversions are:

Event	Section Number
Firstly, there is a brief introduction on how an audit firm is organised – just in case you don't work in this type of organisation.	5.3
All audits must be carried out to high standards of quality – this section explains how that standard is maintained.	5.4
Chapter 4 started the discussion of how much evidence an auditor needs to obtain. This discussion is continued here by introducing the concept of materiality.	5.5
There are different types of evidence that the auditor can use. This section explains the different types of evidence that the auditor can collect and when each type is useful.	5.6
Having decided on the type of evidence to collect, this section explains how much evidence is needed, taking into account materiality and applying the audit risk model.	5.7
Having decided what type of evidence to collect and how many items are needed, statistical sampling is used to determine exactly which items to test (in other words apply audit procedures to).	5.8
Another source of audit evidence is analytical procedures – this section shows the importance of this source of evidence at different stages of the audit.	5.9
All the audit work needs recording in some way; this section explains how to document audit evidence.	5.10
As audit evidence is collected, the auditor may find errors – or misstatements. This section explains how an auditor "deals" with these misstatements.	5.11
In all audits, the auditor must be aware that "special relationships" between individuals and companies may distort the financial statements. This section explains additional audit procedures that are needed on these "related parties".	5.12

	Event	Section Number
✓	Many organisations have internal audit departments. This section explains how the external auditor can place reliance on the work of internal audit.	5.13
	The auditor may also need to obtain advice where specialist knowledge needed on the audit is not available in the audit firm. This section explains how to rely on the work of experts providing that knowledge.	5.14

5.2 So, what is in this chapter?

This chapter is showing you how an audit plan is developed and items selected for audit testing. This is probably the most theoretical chapter in the whole book, but there are some very important points and ISAs to cover. You'll be pleased to know chapters 6 and 7 are very practical as we try and apply all this theory to a "real" audit.

As in chapter 4, many of these sections have an ISA to outline the audit work. As in other chapters, that ISA is summarised and where possible, explained in plain English terms.

5.3 How an audit is organised

To start the chapter, I should let you know who is involved in an audit and what jobs they do.

Any firm providing audit services has a hierarchical structure, with each person in the hierarchy having specific tasks. The exact name for each level in the hierarchy and the exact tasks carried out will vary from firm to firm, but in *general* terms there are five grades of staff each with their own tasks as shown below:

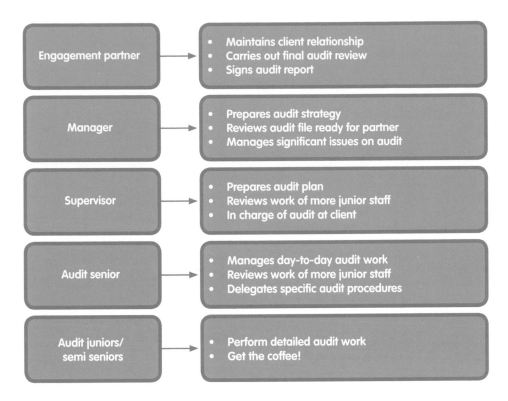

Engagement partner	→	• Maintains client relationship • Carries out final audit review • Signs audit report
Manager	→	• Prepares audit strategy • Reviews audit file ready for partner • Manages significant issues on audit
Supervisor	→	• Prepares audit plan • Reviews work of more junior staff • In charge of audit at client
Audit senior	→	• Manages day-to-day audit work • Reviews work of more junior staff • Delegates specific audit procedures
Audit juniors/ semi seniors	→	• Perform detailed audit work • Get the coffee!

Yes, audit juniors do get the good jobs like locating the coffee machine (trust me, I've been there..).

5.4 Quality control

As you can see from the above section, there are many different staff members on one audit assignment. A small assignment will have at least three staff (partner, manager and junior) while a large one can have hundreds. All those staff need to be co-ordinated and produce work to the same high standard. This is obviously not left to chance; all firms will have some method of maintaining this quality control. There is also an ISA on quality control, which is explained in this section.

Overview of the ISA

ISA 220 *Quality control for an audit of financial statements* explains procedures within an audit firm to maintain quality control of an audit. The ISA also refers to ISQC 1 (*International Standard on Quality Control 1*) which provides a lot more detail on the quality control systems needed within an audit and assurance firm.

ISQC1 standard is not covered in this book; if you are studying audit at an advanced level then you will need to read and understand this standard in addition to ISA 220.

Key things you must understand are:

1. what quality control means, and

2. the importance of the engagement partner in quality control.

These things are explained in the next sections.

Auditor's objectives

The main objective of the auditor with respect to this standard must be to ensure that the audit is carried out in accordance with appropriate quality standards.

The objectives in the ISA therefore are:

d ISA Statement	Plain English statement
The objective of the auditor is to implement quality control procedures at the engagement level that provide the auditor with reasonable assurance that: (a) the audit complies with professional standards and applicable legal and regulatory requirements, and	The audit firm, and therefore each auditor must ensure that audits are carried out to the appropriate quality standard. In other words the auditor must comply with: • professional standards (ISAs, ethical standards and any other standards, issued by their supervising institute) • legal standards (Companies Act or other country specific legislation), and • other regulation such as corporate governance requirements.
(b) the auditor's report issued is appropriate in the circumstances.	Adherence to quality also means that the audit report is correct, so sufficient appropriate audit evidence will be collected and this will support the audit opinion on the financial statements.

Activities in quality control

There are two main "layers" of quality control given in ISA 220. Firstly, the engagement partner is responsible for maintaining quality control throughout the audit. Secondly, a quality control reviewer with no previous connection to the audit will ensure again that quality standards have been maintained.

Here's a summary of the work of the engagement partner regarding quality control:

Responsibility of engagement partner for quality control	Brief explanation
Overall quality control of audit.	So if quality standards are not maintained, it is the engagement partner's fault!
Ensuring audit team follow ethical standards.	Ethical standards were discussed in chapter 2; the engagement partner ensures that these standards are followed by the entire audit team.
Ensuring audit team are independent from client.	The audit team must also show independence from the audit client – this will include, for example, not holding shares in the client. Independence was also discussed in chapter 2.
Ensure that auditor correctly appointed to engagement.	This is a specific requirement to ensure partly that ISA 210 (explained in chapter 4.4) has been complied with and again that the audit firm has no ethical conflicts (e.g. auditing or advising a major competitor).
Audit team have competence to carry out audit work.	The audit firm will provide appropriate training for all staff – there is a requirement for the engagement partner to ensure all grades of staff have received the correct training and so have the skills to carry out the audit.
Direction, review and consultation of the audit work.	These points refer to. • direction : compliance with professional standards • review : Literally review all evidence obtained and ensure it is sufficient and appropriate to support the audit opinion • consultation : that all difficult areas on the audit have been discussed by the audit team and appropriate conclusions drawn from those consultations.
Appointment of the quality control reviewer.	The quality control reviewer is another senior member of the audit firm.

The quality control reviewer will then effectively repeat some of the quality control checks carried out by the engagement partner. The benefit of using the reviewer is that they will not have been involved in the audit but will effectively re-check the application of quality control from an objective viewpoint.

- Reviewing significant judgements of audit team.

- Check audit firm is independent from client.

- Ensure that the audit team/client have discussed audit problems.

- Ensure documentation produced reflects the audit work carried out.

So that is quality control; the audit must be carried out in accordance with quality control standards so that the opinion is trusted.

5.5 Materiality

Materiality is a concept that auditors use to try to determine how significant something is within the financial statements. The auditor normally uses some measure of materiality in determining which items to test and in evaluating the results or errors found during testing. ISA 320 *Materiality in planning and performing an audit* is the relevant ISA.

Overview of the ISA

The ISA explains the concept of materiality and how it can be used on an audit. However, don't expect any absolute measures; the ISA is clear in stating that determining an amount for materiality is a matter for the judgement of the auditor.

Key things you must understand are:

1. what materiality is, and

2. how to calculate it.

These things are explained in the next sections.

Auditor's objectives

The overall objective of the auditor is to try and ensure that the financial statements are free of material misstatement.

There is one objective in this ISA:

d ISA Statement	Plain English statement
The objective of the auditor is to apply the concept of materiality appropriately in planning and performing the audit.	All this means is that the auditor must be aware of materiality at all times. Audit work will generally be directed to the material items and any errors found, evaluated according to how serious or "large" they are in the context of the financial statements.

What is materiality?

A good question – and to be fair quite a difficult one to answer. In fact the ISA mentions two different types of materiality.

1. **Materiality**. This is the amount where a change to any figure in the financial statements would influence the economic decisions of users taken on the basis of those financial statements. In other words, if you were thinking about buying shares in a company, then materiality is the amount by which profit for the year (for example) would have to change before you would decide not to invest.

The ISA also correctly points out that for some figures in the financial statements a lower level of materiality is appropriate. The normal example here is director's remuneration. You would expect this to be accurately stated – and so materiality is likely to be a matter of a few $s, not thousands or millions.

2. **Performance materiality**. This figure is less than materiality. This is the amount used by the auditor in planning and performing audit procedures. If performance materiality is exceeded (that is the auditor finds errors above this amount), then there is more than a "low" risk that there are *material* uncorrected errors or misstatements in the financial statements.

Got that? Materiality is the amount that affects the users; performance materiality is the guideline amount that the auditor uses. The difference between materiality and the lower performance materiality is determined by the auditor's skill and judgement.

Finally, the ISA also states that materiality can be revised as the audit progresses. This will happen where the auditor discovers information which indicates the initial materiality determination was wrong.

Are there any guides to what materiality could be?

Another good question. The answer is yes, but again don't expect any precise answers.

Typical amounts for materiality include:

Benchmark for materiality	Example or guide to the materiality figure
Profit before tax (for continuing operations of the entity)	Can be used for profit orientated entities. More than 5% is the suggested amount for a manufacturing company.
Gross profit	Profit orientated entities where profit before tax can vary significantly. No % suggested in the ISA.
Turnover	More than 1% for a not-for-profit company although is also used in profit making companies.

Of course, the auditor's skill and judgement will be used to determine the exact amount for materiality; these are only guidelines.

 In 27/4Books

In 27/4Books, net profit before taxation is $277,000 – so 5% of this figure would be $13,850. This appears to be a low amount; would users really be affected by profit or sales for example being incorrect by this amount? Possibly not. Remember 27/4Books is not a manufacturing company – a higher amount such as 1% of turnover ($11,023,000 * 1%) or $110,023 may be more applicable; however, this could be considered too high. The auditor may therefore use judgement and decide on say $50,000 as materiality.

This would mean performance materiality will be set below this figure – perhaps at $40,000 – although again the auditor's judgement would be used to decide this.

5.6 Detailed audit plan - evidence collection

Having carried out a risk assessment and agreed a materiality level for the audit, the auditor can delay no longer – audit evidence must now be collected to find out whether there are any material misstatements in the financial statements. ISA 330 *The auditor's responses to assessed risks* is the relevant ISA here.

Overview of the ISA

The ISA explains the general approach to collecting evidence and the methods of evidence collection. There is quite a lot of detail in the ISA so this section summarises the key points, but with a focus on providing an understanding of evidence collection and bearing in mind the need to answer examination questions on this topic.

Key things you must understand are:

1. the overview of how risk assessment is linked to audit evidence collection

2. the different methods of collecting audit evidence and when they are used, and

3. what the ISA states explicitly about the different methods of collecting evidence.

These things are explained in the next sections.

Auditor's objectives

The overall objective of the auditor is to obtain sufficient appropriate audit evidence – as the ISA says.

d ISA Statement	Plain English statement
The objective of the auditor is to obtain sufficient appropriate audit evidence regarding the assessed risks of material misstatement, through designing and implementing appropriate responses to those risks.	The ISA is fairly clear I think. The auditor needs to collect audit evidence (that is the appropriate response to the risks) to make a decision on whether or not there are material misstatements in the financial statements.

Method of obtaining sufficient appropriate audit evidence

What the auditor aims to do is collect audit evidence with the objective of forming an opinion that there are no material misstatements in the financial statements being audited. This means that there will be a detailed audit plan for each identified risk. For example, there is the risk that sales are not complete in the financial statements. There will be an audit plan to obtain evidence to try and ensure sales are complete. Chapters 6 and 7 provide example risks and the normal audit procedures (in other words those procedures that the audit plan requires to be used).

For each of these identified risks, the auditor will carry out a 4-step process as follows:

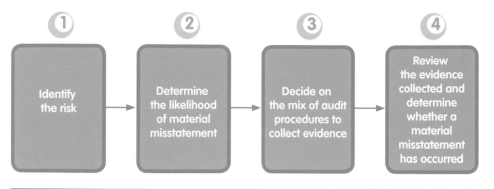

Step	Comment
①	Specific risks are identified, such as the risk of lack of completeness of income, as noted above.
②	How likely a material misstatement is for each risk will be determined. Here, the auditor reviews the inherent risk relating to the specific risk identified and then the control risk regarding the effectiveness of the control systems. This will give the balance of detection risk and therefore an indication of how much audit evidence needs to be collected. (see chapter 4.8 on the interaction between the different types of risk).
③	The auditor now decides on the method of collecting audit evidence. There are three main methods of collecting evidence (see below) and the mix of these methods will be decided.
④	Finally, when evidence collection is complete, the auditor will decide whether or not a material misstatement has occurred. This decision is based on the errors, if any, found during evidence collection.

As already mentioned, the detail on evidence collection for the Income Statement and Statement of Financial Position is explained in chapters 6 and 7.

Methods of collecting audit evidence

The auditor has three main methods of collecting audit evidence. They are:

- substantive procedures, which comprise two separate procedures called

    - substantive analytical procedures and

    - tests of detail, and

- tests of controls.

These procedures are explained in the table below, along with a brief example of when they are used. As already mentioned above, chapters 6 and 7 provide lots of examples of audit procedures.

Audit procedure	Explanation	Used when	Example in 27/4Books
Substantive analytical procedures	Comparing financial and non-financial information to try to determine its overall accuracy.	The auditor needs to ensure some figures are reasonably correct in the financial statements.	The total salaries expenditure can be verified by finding the number of staff paid a salary, multiplied by the average salary.
Tests of detail	The auditor tests audit assertions by tracing documents through that system or testing a Statement of Financial Position (SFP) balance.	Where tests of control are not possible or where results of testing need to be evaluated in monetary terms.	Tracing despatch notes to sales invoices (see section 6.6) or testing the completeness of the receivables balance (see section 7.8).
Test of controls	Ensure controls are operating correctly.	The auditor decides to rely on controls to decrease substantive testing. OR Substantive procedures cannot provide sufficient audit evidence for a particular risk.	Examining a despatch note to ensure it has been signed as evidence of a control being applied (see section 6.6).

These procedures are then used throughout the audit. However, most audits are divided into two main stages being the interim and final audits. The types of procedures used in each stage are shown below:

Stage of audit	Timing	Procedures used
Interim	Normally before the year end.	Detailed testing on transactions that will form the Income Statement (IS) (sales, purchases etc.) using: • substantive analytical procedures • tests of details • tests of controls.
Final	After the year end – the Statement of Financial Position must be available for audit.	Update any transaction testing to the year-end AND Testing of the balances on the SFP using: • substantive analytical procedures, and • tests of details. Note tests of controls are not normally used here because the SFP does not accumulate transactions.

Note therefore that substantive procedures can be used throughout the entire audit (including testing of the IS and SFP) but tests of controls are normally used to test the IS.

More detail on substantive procedures

The ISA contains a lot more advice about the use of substantive procedures – I've summarised this into a question and answer table so you can see the important points quickly.

Question	Answer
Does the auditor have to use substantive procedures?	Yes- the ISA states clearly that substantive procedures must be performed for each material balance in the financial statements – even though the risk of material misstatement may be low.
Is the evidence for substantive procedures always obtained from the client's accounting systems?	No – sometimes direct confirmations are used – evidence is obtained from third parties. Examples of this evidence include receivable confirmations and valuation of buildings (see chapter 7 for examples of this type of evidence).
Are there any substantive procedures that must be performed?	Yes – the ISA states that the auditor must ensure that balances in the financial statements are represented by the accounting system at the client and all material journal entries from accounts preparation must be reviewed.
When are substantive procedures performed?	During the interim and final audits. Where substantive procedures are used on an interim audit, then the auditor will normally perform more testing on the final audit to cover the period from the interim audit to the date of the financial statements.
What happens if errors are found during testing?	The audit will either: attempt to obtain more evidence by testing more items, OR where sufficient evidence cannot be obtained, produce a qualified opinion on the financial statements.

More detail on analytical procedures is provided in section 5.9 below.

More detail on tests of controls

The ISA also contains a lot more advice about the use of tests of control – as with substantive procedures here's a table with the key points.

Question	Answer
How initially does the auditor find out whether controls are working correctly?	By asking management.
When are controls normally tested?	Testing normally takes place during the year being audited – for example if the client's year-end is 31 December 20X0, then controls must be tested in the period 1 January to 31 December 20X0.
Are there any situations where reliance is being placed on controls but those controls do not have to be tested?	Yes, where controls do not change, then the auditor can decide to rely on audit testing from previous years and simply ask management this year to confirm that controls are operating effectively. However, each control must be tested at least once every three years.
But surely some controls must be tested each year?	Yes, key controls must be tested every year.
What happens if errors are found during testing – that is controls have not been applied correctly?	The auditor must find out why the control was not applied by asking management and client staff. Then the auditor needs to determine: 1. sufficient evidence has been obtained, OR 2. whether additional evidence is necessary (as in carrying out more testing of that control), OR 3. whether more substantive testing is required to find out whether there is a misstatement.

Conclusion on audit evidence

You should now be familiar with why an auditor collects audit evidence and the types of evidence that can be collected. As mentioned throughout this section, chapters 6 and 7 provide the detail on evidence collection so when you read these sections, think back to this section; it should make the reason for collecting evidence clearer.

5.7 Audit evidence

Discussion so far has been on the need to collect audit evidence, but not really explaining what that evidence is. The next ISA comes to the rescue here detailing not only what evidence to collect but which sort of evidence. This is ISA 500 which is called, not surprisingly, *Audit evidence*.

Overview of the ISA

The ISA explains that the auditor must collect enough (or sufficient) evidence and that this evidence must be both relevant and reliable. There are plenty of examples of these terms in the ISA, which is also important from the examination point of view. If you are taking examinations in auditing, there are a few important lists to learn, as you will see later.

Key things you must understand are:

1. the overview of how risk assessment is linked to audit evidence collection

2. the different methods of collecting audit evidence and when they are used, and

3. what the ISA states explicitly about the different methods of collecting evidence.

These things are explained in the next sections.

Auditor's objectives

The overall objective of the auditor is to obtain sufficient appropriate audit evidence – as the ISA says.

d ISA Statement	Plain English statement
The objective of the auditor is to design and perform audit procedures in such a way as to enable the auditor to obtain sufficient appropriate audit evidence to be able to draw reasonable conclusions on which to base the auditor's opinion.	The ISA seems fairly clear. But to re-state; the auditor must collect enough audit evidence to support the audit opinion on the financial statements. That evidence will be collected using recognised audit procedures.

This objective contains the key words of sufficient and appropriate which I'll explain below.

Sufficient and appropriate evidence

In terms of audit evidence:

* "sufficiency" refers to the quantity or amount of the evidence obtained

* "appropriate" refers to the quality of the evidence obtained. In terms of quality this means that evidence must be relevant and reliable.

Remember that ISA 200 requires the auditor

> to obtain sufficient appropriate audit evidence to reduce audit risk to an acceptably low level, and thereby enable the auditor to draw reasonable conclusions on which to base the auditor's opinion.

ISA 500 is therefore saying that the auditor must get enough evidence of the correct quality to meet this objective.

We therefore need to find out:

1. what is meant by appropriate evidence?

2. what makes that evidence relevant?, and

3. what types of evidence are reliable?

The next three sections answer these questions.

Appropriate evidence

To be appropriate, evidence has to be obtained using a recognised audit procedure. The ISA lists 7 possible audit procedures, as shown in the following table. For each procedure I've included the normal "plain English" statement and an example of that procedure in terms of test of controls or substantive procedure. Gaps in these columns indicate that the audit procedure is not normally used as either a test of control or substantive procedure.

⚷ Audit procedure	ISA statement	Plain English statement	Test of control	Substantive procedure
Inspection	Inspection involves examining records or documents, whether internal or external, in paper form, electronic form or other media, or a physical examination of an asset.	Inspection means to examine or scrutinise something. In the context of audit procedures inspection therefore means that the auditor will obtain some evidence such as a document or computer record and review that document for specific evidence.	Looking at a document for evidence of a signature.	Obtaining the title deeds of a property as evidence of ownership.
Observation	Observation consists of looking at a process or procedure being performed by others, for example, the auditor's observation of inventory counting by the entity's personnel, or of the performance of control activities.	Observation means to watch or inspect something. However, observation tests are limited because they only provide evidence of controls or procedures at the time of observation. Procedures may be different at other times simply because people tend to change their actions when not observed.	Observing staff arriving for work and confirming their attendance by signing an attendance sheet.	

Audit procedure	ISA statement	Plain English statement	Test of control	Substantive procedure
External confirmation	An external confirmation represents audit evidence obtained by the auditor as a direct written response to the auditor from a third party (the confirming party), in paper form, or by electronic or other medium.	An external confirmation means literally to obtain information from a third party, normally in written format. This is good audit evidence because the third party is independent of the client which normally increases the reliability of the evidence.		Obtaining letters from receivables to confirm that receivable exists – see chapter 7.8
Recalculation	Recalculation consists of checking the mathematical accuracy of documents or records. Recalculation may be performed manually or electronically.	Re-calculation means literally that – the mathematical accuracy of accounting or other records is checked to ensure that any totals are correct.		Adding up the individual sales in the sales day book to ensure that the day book total is correct.
Reperformance	Reperformance involves the auditor's independent execution of procedures or controls that were originally performed as part of the entity's internal control.	The auditor literally repeats actions that have already been performed within the company's accounting systems simply to make sure that those actions were carried out correctly.	If there is a signature on the invoice confirming that the transfer has been checked then this confirms that the control has been applied.	Details on a despatch note are agreed to the sales invoice. This confirms that the details were correct.

⚲ Audit procedure	ISA statement	Plain English statement	Test of control	Substantive procedure
Analytical procedures	Analytical procedures consist of evaluations of financial information through analysis of plausible relationships among both financial and non-financial data.	Analytical procedures have their own ISA – 520. Please see section 5.9 in this chapter for more details.		
Inquiry	Inquiry consists of seeking information of knowledgeable persons, both financial and non-financial, within the entity or outside the entity.	Here the auditor asks questions of management or other people in the company or outside of it. The evidence obtained may be oral or may be documented – the latter being more reliable.	Management are asked to confirm the features of a new control system are working correctly.	Management are asked to explain why sales have increased.

How to remember the list? The first letters of the procedures are: I O E R R AP I. I've thought about memory joggers for a while – how about if you are a poor student in debt and want to qualify as an auditor quickly?

- I
- Owe
- Errr
- Rapid
- Results
- APpreciated
- by I

Relevant evidence

(Remember that appropriate evidence means relevant and reliable - these terms are now explained). "Relevance" means that the evidence being collected must relate to an audit procedure and the assertion that procedure is being used to test.

For example:

- relevant evidence to ensure that inventory exists is seeing that inventory
- relevant evidence to ensure that accounts payable exist is seeing purchase invoices and/or statements from the payable.

But, if the auditor attempted to review the computerised inventory records of a company to confirm existence of inventory this would not be relevant evidence because looking at a computer system does not actually show the inventory exists.

So that's it; relevant evidence is simply evidence that satisfactorily tests the assertion being considered.

Reliable evidence

"Reliability" in terms of audit evidence refers to how much confidence the audit has that the evidence can be trusted. Trust in turn depends on the source of the evidence. For example, if you are ill you will probably ask a doctor for a diagnosis rather than a used car salesman. While both people could tell you what is wrong, the doctor is more likely to be correct because of the training received. In this sense the doctor provides reliable evidence.

The ISA provides 5 guidelines as to what constitutes reliable evidence; here they are:

More reliable evidence	Less reliable evidence	Comment
Obtained from independent sources outside the entity.	Obtained from sources within the entity.	In most situations, evidence from outside the entity is more reliable because there is less likelihood of fraud or misstatement. For example, management could "hide" liabilities but a company owed money would want to be repaid.
Internal evidence where controls over preparation and maintenance are effective.	Internal evidence with no control over preparation or maintenance.	A good internal control system will mean the data in that system is more reliable. For example, a sales invoice will be signed to confirm the accuracy of the additions.
Obtained directly by the auditor.	Obtained indirectly or by inference.	An audit procedure such as observing a control is working is more reliable than simply asking management whether that control works, without actually seeing the control in action.
Obtained in documentary form, whether paper, electronic, or other medium.	Obtained orally.	Documentary evidence can be looked at again to confirm what the evidence actually says; however, words cannot be "seen" again.
Provided by original documents.	Provided by photocopies or facsimiles, or documents that have been filmed, digitized or otherwise transformed into electronic form.	The accuracy of any document which is copied depends on the integrity of the copying process. The copying process may therefore be incomplete or in some situations the process itself can create invalid documents (e.g. photocopying a signature from one document onto another).

A point on obtaining audit evidence

The auditor is allowed to use evidence from more than one source. If the conclusions from both sources of evidence agree with each other, then the overall level of assurance obtained increases. Obviously, if the results from two sources of evidence are different then the auditor must find out why this difference has occurred.

So that's audit evidence for you. Next is audit sampling, to decide which items to select for testing.

5.8 Audit or Statistical sampling

When selecting items for testing, the auditor needs to ensure that there is little or no bias in that selection – that is where statistical sampling comes in. ISA 530 *Audit sampling* is the relevant ISA here.

Overview of the ISA

This ISA explains how an auditor can choose a sample of items from a population for testing, eliminating as much bias as possible from that selection. Other selection methods are also mentioned to give a complete list of sampling methods available to the auditor.

Key things you must understand are:

1. what statistical sampling is

2. how to obtain a sample from a population, and

3. the different methods of obtaining a sample.

These things are explained in the next sections.

Auditor's objectives

The overall objective of the auditor is to try ensure that the financial statements are free of material misstatement.

There is only one objective in this ISA:

![d] ISA Statement	Plain English statement
The objective of the auditor, when using audit sampling, is to provide a reasonable basis for the auditor to draw conclusions about the population from which the sample is selected.	The aim of audit sampling is to ensure that the auditor collects sufficient evidence to draw conclusions about the population being tested. Conclusions in this sense include whether there are errors in the population and where possible whether these errors result in a material misstatement.

What is statistical sampling?

Good question. There are two characteristics of sample selection that must be adhered to before it can be termed statistical:

1. random selection of the sample items, and

2. the use of probability theory to evaluate sample results.

In other words, items to be sampled must be selected without bias which also means that the results from sampling can be analysed statistically to show the effect on the total population.

When selecting items for testing, the auditor is also subject to sampling risk and non-sampling risk. These risks have already been explained in section 4.8.

Obtaining a statistical sample

Let's say you need to select a sample of items for testing – that is you know:

- what the total population of something like despatch notes is (perhaps 20,000 for the year), and

- that 45 items are needed for testing (taking into account inherent risk, control risk and materiality).

Here's a summary of the 8 steps you must go through to carry out the test. I've used the example of despatch notes in the table after the diagram to try and show how sampling works on an audit.

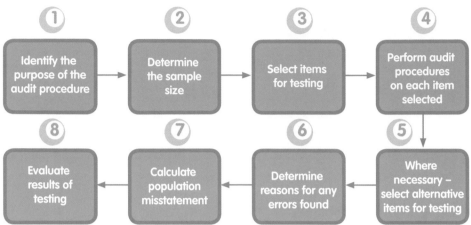

Step	Commentary	ⓔ Example
①	The auditor must know the objective of the audit procedure to ensure that statistical sampling is appropriate and so an error can be identified, should it occur.	All goods despatch notes result in a sales invoice being produced.
②	The sample size must be set to lower sampling risk to an acceptable level. The size will be determined by the auditor's statistical sampling methodology. Sampling risk has already been mentioned in section 4.8.	45 despatch notes could be chosen – the auditor will have determined that at this level, the sample results will accurately reflect the population result.
③	With statistical sampling each item must have an equal chance of being selected. With non-statistical sampling the auditor uses skill and judgement to select the items for testing.	Random number tables or a computer program generating random numbers will select the items for testing. The auditor enters the first and last despatch note numbers used for the year into the program and the program provides the random despatch note numbers for testing.

(4) The chosen items are tested! The despatch notes are found and their details agreed to the relevant sales invoices.

(5) In a limited number of situations, the chosen items are not available for testing so alternative items will have to be chosen.

In the sample, one despatch note was cancelled because the order was cancelled – an alternative despatch note is selected or the objective of the procedure of matching despatch note details to invoices cannot be met.

(6) If errors occur, the reasons for those errors must be identified. Normally errors indicate a weakness in the company systems and the sample size will be increased to try to find the extent of the error. Very occasionally, errors are an "anomaly" – that is they occurred for a very good reason and are unlikely to occur again; these errors can be ignored.

On one despatch note, the quantity of books sold was incorrectly recorded on the invoice (9 books were despatched but 10 were recorded on the invoice). This appeared to be a computer program error and 15 more items were selected for testing to try to determine the extent of the error; however, no other errors were found.

(7) Where the sampling unit relates to a control or substantive test of detail, then the population error will be proportional to the sample error rate.

As noted on the left, this is a test of detail – reperforming the transfer of data from a despatch note to the sales invoice.

Where the sampling unit is a monetary value then the value can be placed on the population error.

The error rate is 1 item in 60 (that's the 45 items testing at first and then the additional 15 from step 6 above) which is likely to be the population error.

(8) High error rates can indicate that a material misstatement may occur. The auditor will need to determine how likely a material error actually is.

An error rate of 1 in 60 appears high – although the error should also be detected by client staff or by the customer not paying the invoice as the goods invoice exceeds the goods despatched. The auditor may therefore conclude that there is no material misstatement, but still continue to investigate the error – especially if it was caused by a computer program.

With control testing and tests of details it is not possible to quantify the error as the sampling unit is a document, not a monetary value.

So that's how you carry out a statistical sample. One other small thing to mention; you may have noted that the population size was hardly discussed in determining the sample. This is because in statistical terms the size of the population has almost no effect on the sample size. A relatively low number of items will be chosen whether the population is 1,000 or 1,000,000 items. Only a limited number of items have to be chosen to ensure that the sample does have the same characteristics as the whole population.

Types of sampling

The ISA mentions various types of sampling methods. Here's a summary of those methods, partly so you have a complete list and partly because examination questions ask for the different methods of sampling. Note that haphazard and block are not statistical methods of sampling.

Sampling method	Brief explanation
Random selection	Selection using random number generators. The number of items in a population is found and the number of items to test. A random number generator provides random items to test in that population eliminating any bias.
Systematic selection	Sample size is divided by the number of units to sample (e.g. 10,000 / 50) to give a sampling interval (here of 200). After using a random start, such as item 150, each 200th item is tested (350, 550 etc.). This method is not random and may have bias.
Monetary unit sampling (MUS)	The sampling unit is the $ in the account balance rather than the number of items (as in random selection). For example, in a receivables balance of $1,753,000, random selection is used to choose 25 individual "$" from $1 to $1,753,000, in that balance. The receivables balance containing each $ is tested. MUS focuses attention on larger items as large balances have a higher chance of selection (they contain more individual "$"'s).
Haphazard selection	The auditor selects the items for testing using skill and judgement and attempting to avoid any bias. While unusual items may be selected, this method is not random.
Block selection	Selection of a contiguous block of items in a whole population. For example, all transactions in the month of May could be selected for testing. This method is not random with the specific weakness that testing one block only effectively ignores the rest of the population and any errors that could be there.

Other concepts	Explanation
Stratification	This is dividing the population of items in sub-groups; for example dividing a receivables balance by value (all items above $100,000 then those between $50,000 and $99,999 and finally any below $49,999. Audit procedures can be applied to each sub-group but now larger items are automatically chosen meaning that more of the value of the population is tested.
Sampling unit	The item to be selected for sampling.
Population	The total number of items to be available for testing.

We now know how to apply statistical sampling to determine which items to test and how to evaluate errors. Next up are analytical procedures, the other part of substantive testing which have their own ISA.

5.9 Analytical Procedures

Analytical Procedures are used at various stages in the audit as a guide to confirm whether or not figures in the financial statements are roughly correct. ISA 520 *Analytical procedures* is the relevant ISA here.

Overview of the ISA

This ISA explains how an auditor should use analytical procedures as part of collecting evidence on an audit. Technically, I should be discussing analytical procedures after a more detailed explanation of risk assessment as outlined previously in ISA330. However, analytical procedures tend to "fit" quite nicely into this part of the book. ISA330 will be discussed shortly.

Key things you must understand are:

1. what analytical procedures are, and

2. how analytical procedures are used.

These things are explained in the next sections.

Auditor's objectives

The overall objective of the auditor is to try and ensure that the financial statements are free of material misstatement.

The auditor's objectives from the ISA are:

d ISA Statement	Plain English statement
To obtain relevant and reliable audit evidence when using substantive analytical procedures.	The auditor will collect audit evidence using "substantive analytical procedures" – which basically means ensuring that figures in the financial statements meet with the auditor's expectations, normally at the beginning of the audit.
To design and perform analytical procedures near the end of the audit that assist the auditor when forming an overall conclusion as to whether the financial statements are consistent with the auditor's understanding of the entity.	Then at the end of the audit, again ensure that the figures in the financial statements agree with the other evidence collected by the auditor. See chapter 8 for detail on the final review of financial statements.

Timing of analytical procedures

To be clear, the ISA indicates that analytical procedures can be used at different stages during the audit:

1. at the beginning of the audit and during the audit as Substantive Analytical Procedures

2. at the end of the audit.

This section explains the first use of analytical procedures; as mentioned above, the use of analytical procedures at the end of the audit is explained in chapter 8.

Stages of performing Substantive Analytical Procedures

When an auditor uses analytical procedures at the beginning of or during an audit, the ISA actually refers to these as Substantive Analytical Procedures (SAP). This is because the auditor is obtaining independent evidence to verify figures in the financial statements. Evidence collection in the context of ISA530 was explained in more detail in section 5.6.

There are four stages to carry out effective analytical procedures:

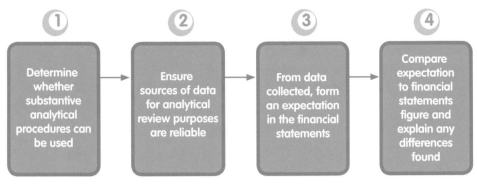

Stage	Explanation
①	Substantive Analytical Procedures (SAP) are normally used where there are large numbers of transactions or where amounts are easy to predict. For example, the sales figure is normally used with SAP (see example below) along with salaries (number of staff * average salary should give the salary expense).
②	SAP rely on evidence being available to verify figures independently from the accounting systems. For example, salaries would be verified from personnel records. The auditor needs to ensure that this independent data is available.
③	From the data collected, the auditor must be able to calculate roughly what the financial statements figure will be. For example, personnel records will give number of salaried staff and salary rates hence the salary charge in the financial statements can be calculated.
④	Finally, the expected amount just calculated is compared to the financial statements figure. If the figures are roughly the same then the auditor has confirmed that the financial statements figure is about correct; if the two figures are different then more work will be needed to understand why they are different. There is now the possibility of a misstatement in the financial statements.

Income statement – 27/4Books

Let's have a look at some analytical procedures in practice. Here's the income statement for 27/4Books – not yet audited, but hopefully fairly accurate as the management of 27/4Books have prepared it.

27/4Books Ltd
Income Statement

	52 Weeks ended	52 Weeks ended
	30 Dec 20X1	31 Dec 20X0
	$'000	$'000
Sales	11,023	9,557
Cost of Sales	7,923	6,217
Gross profit	3,100	3,340
Administration costs	1,602	1,557
Selling and distribution costs	1,221	1,524
Net profit before taxation	277	259
Taxation	95	87
Net profit after taxation	182	172

Let's assume that our evidence collection so far has shown that:

- management indicate that 27/4Books has had a good trading year

- 27/4Books obtained three significant clients during the year, and

- industry figures indicate that book sales increased by 12%.

From this information we should expect 27/4Books sales to have increased more than the industry average because of the "good trading year" and the increase in the client base. In fact sales have increased by 15% which meets our expectations.

However, if sales have increased, then we would also expect selling and distribution costs to increase because if more books are sold, then transport costs increase. Similarly, obtaining new clients probably meant additional selling costs in obtaining those clients. So from the SAP point of view, we are expecting selling and distribution costs to increase about 15% in line with sales.

Is this the case? No, selling and distribution costs are only 80% of the previous year's figure – the costs have fallen. Strange. Further investigation will be necessary to find out why the costs are lower. No, I don't have the answer but this is an example of where SAP helps direct the audit procedures to risky areas where a misstatement may have occurred.

What if analytical procedures are inconclusive?

In situations, like the example above, where analytical procedures indicate the possibility of error, the auditor will:

- ask management to try and explain the difference, and

- obtain other audit evidence – normally from substantive testing – tests of details.

Remember substantive testing – tests of details, was explained in section 5.6.

5.10 Audit documentation

The auditor needs to record audit work in some way. Recording in this context means writing things down, whether on paper or electronically. This record of the audit becomes, not surprisingly, audit documentation.

Overview of the ISA

The need for, and the contents of, audit documentation are contained in ISA 230 *Audit documentation*. This is a very straightforward ISA listing many common sense points about recording audit evidence and then having this evidence available for review both during and after the completion of the audit.

Key things you must understand are:

1. why audit documentation is produced

2. the benefits of producing audit documentation, and

3. the typical contents of audit documentation.

These things are explained in the next sections.

Auditor's objectives

The auditor's objective is literally to ensure that all documentation required to support the audit opinion is available in the audit file.

The specific objectives that the auditor must follow are:

d ISA Statement	Plain English statement
The objective of the auditor is to prepare documentation that provides: (a) a sufficient and appropriate record of the basis for the auditor's report, and (b) evidence that the audit was planned and performed in accordance with ISAs and applicable legal and regulatory requirements.	The auditor's report (and therefore any opinion that report gives) must be supported by appropriate audit evidence – or audit documentation. The documentation must also show that the auditor followed all relevant laws and regulations. This will be mainly the ISAs but some countries may also have other laws which must also be followed.

The actual format of audit documentation is not prescribed, although the ISA does assume that there will be an audit file and that audit documentation will be arranged within this file in some logical sequence.

Why produce audit documentation?

Apart from providing evidence to refer back to at a later date, other reasons for producing audit documentation include:

1. helping the auditor plan the audit – the documentation providing the plan

2. providing audit evidence to show work is being carried out in accordance with the plan and allowing managers and partners to review the evidence obtained.

3. showing which member of the audit team produced which documents, so it is known who is responsible for those documents

4. providing evidence to help plan future audits

5. providing evidence that quality control standards have been maintained

6. providing evidence that the auditor has complied with ISAs and other regulations.

This is another useful list from the examination point of view.

Audit documentation – typical contents

The other useful thing to know about audit documentation is the typical contents of an audit file. So an audit file normally contains:

1. a record of all audit procedures carried out to show compliance with the ISAs

2. the results of those procedures and a record of the evidence obtained, and

3. the matters that occurred during the audit, how those matters were resolved and the auditor's reasons for reaching those conclusions.

Again, these three things are useful to know in an auditing examination.

5.11 Action to take on misstatements

As noted earlier in this chapter, the auditor may find misstatements as the audit progresses. ISA 450 *Evaluation of misstatements identified during the audit* explains what to do with those misstatements.

Overview of the ISA

This ISA explains what the auditor needs to do when misstatements are found, linking back to the need to amend the audit strategy and forward to the ISAs on audit reporting.

Key things you must understand are:

1. the auditor's objectives regarding misstatements,

2. the different types of misstatements, and

3. audit procedures for evaluating misstatements.

However, as misstatements are evaluated at the end of the audit, I'll defer talking about these until chapter 8 when all of the activities towards the end of the audit are discussed. Just remember for now please that misstatements may be found during audit testing (which is discussed in chapters 6 and 7) and how to deal with those misstatements is contained in chapter 8.

5.12 Special audit work – related parties

In some situations, one or more parties may be able to exert significant control over a company either because they own shares in that company or because they have management control of that company. These groups are therefore in a position to either affect strategy or obtain beneficial terms of trade with the company. This means that there is a possibility of material misstatement because transactions are not recorded correctly, or some benefit has been given to the related party rather than the company.

Overview of the ISA

ISA 550 *Related parties* explains how an auditor can identify related parties and then seek out transactions which may have been affected by those related parties.

The ISA is very detailed and so this section only provides a summary. If you are studying auditing at an advanced level then you will need to study the ISA itself in much more detail.

Key things you must understand are:

1. what the auditor's objectives are regarding related parties

2. what audit work is carried out to identify related parties

3. who are related parties anyway, and

4. how information on related parties is disclosed in the financial statements.

These things are explained in the next sections.

Auditor's objectives

As always, the objective of the auditor is to ensure that the opinion on the financial statements is correct. The auditor is therefore concerned that related parties may deliberately or otherwise cause financial statements to include material misstatements,

The actual objectives in this ISA are quite lengthy:

d ISA Statement	Plain English statement
(i) To recognise fraud risk factors, if any, arising from related party relationships and transactions that are relevant to the identification and assessment of the risks of material misstatement due to fraud, and	The auditor must understand that financial statements may contain misstatements caused by related parties – and this could include fraud – deliberate misstatements.
(ii) To conclude, based on the audit evidence obtained, whether the financial statements, insofar as they are affected by those relationships and transactions: a. achieve fair presentation (for fair presentation frameworks), or b. are not misleading (for compliance frameworks).	Sufficient evidence must therefore be obtained to confirm that the financial statements are materially correct including presentation of information and not just the amount of any transactions.
Where the applicable financial reporting framework establishes related party requirements, to obtain sufficient appropriate audit evidence about whether related party relationships and transactions have been appropriately identified, accounted for and disclosed in the financial statements in accordance with the framework.	Also, where there are specific regulations or laws regarding related party transactions, that those regulations and laws have been complied with in the financial statements being audited. Again enough audit evidence must be obtained to make this determination

Auditor's work on related party transactions

Audit work on related party transactions really continues throughout the whole of the audit engagement – there is not really any specific time when the auditor effectively sits down and says "OK – today I'm going to find related party transactions."

The auditor will work on related party transactions when some event indicates work is needed on this area. In summary though, the ISA recommends audit work is performed as follows:

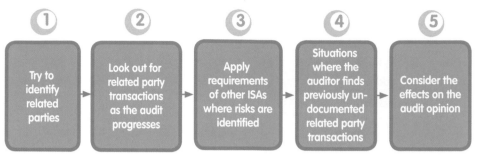

Step	Commentary
①	Identification of related parties will include asking management how they identify related parties and ensuring all appropriate disclosures of related party transactions have been made in the financial statements.
②	Key evidence in this respect includes large/unusual bank transactions, large unusual transactions and shareholders' and directors' meeting minutes.
③	ISA 315 requires that the auditor assess risks of material misstatement and ISA 240 identifies risk factors regarding fraud. These ISAs are explained in sections 4.6 and 4.9.
④	The auditor will have to update the audit team with this information then: • inform management, finding out why the transactions had not been disclosed previously • perform more audit procedures to find out how significant the transactions are, and • consider whether or not the audit strategy is affected and needs possible amendment.
⑤	Finally, if related party transactions are not disclosed correctly (in monetary or wording terms), that is specific details about related parties are not provided in the financial statements, the auditor will need to consider whether to amend the audit report. ISA 700 applies here (see chapter 9).

Who are related parties?

So you know, related parties can include the following:

Related party	Example
i. People or entities having direct or indirect equity holdings or other financial interests in the entity.	A company holding shares in another company (particularly when this gives associated or subsidiary company status).
ii. The company being audited holds, directly or indirectly, equity or other financial interests in other entities.	The company under audit has purchased shares in other companies, especially where associated or subsidiary companies.
iii. A member of management or those charged with governance.	This includes directors (executive and non-executive) as they have the responsibility for running the company.
iv. Close family members of any person in category iii above.	This definition of "family member" will vary by country but will normally include spouse and minor children. So if a child holds shares in a company, the parent becomes the related party.
v. The company having a significant business relationship with any person referred to in category iii above.	This could include business partners – so a director of a company could be running a separate business with another person – that person therefore becomes a related party.

Disclosure of related party transactions

Financial statement disclosures for related parties vary from country to country. Disclosure requirements may be set by statute, corporate governance regulations or simply "best practice".

For example, in the UK, the Companies Act 2006 has some disclosure provisions, while the Combined Code contains other recommendations. You will need to investigate the specific requirements for your country

5.13 Reliance on internal audit

There are some situations where the external auditor may be able to rely on the work of the internal auditor.

Overview of the ISA

ISA 610 *Using the work of internal auditors* explains how the external auditor places this reliance. Note though that the ISA relates only to situations where the external auditor wants to rely on the existing work of the internal auditor; if the external auditor specifically asks the internal auditor for assistance, for example in carrying out some of the external auditors procedures that work is outside the scope of the ISA.

Key things you must understand are:

1. the auditor's objectives regarding placing reliance on internal audit

2. how to decide when reliance can be placed on internal audit

3. the effect on the auditor's work having placed reliance, and

4. how to ensure that the work produced by internal audit is actually reliable.

These things are explained in the next sections.

Auditor's objectives

We know that the objective of the auditor is to obtain sufficient reliable audit evidence to form an opinion on the financial statements. The auditor obtains evidence from various sources to support that opinion and one source can be the work of internal audit. The auditor will therefore need to decide whether to use internal audit work and if so whether that work is of a sufficient standard to place reliance on it.

Remember, even if the internal audit work is used, the external auditor will not be able to refer to this in the audit report; any such reference could imply that the external auditor delegated some responsibility to the internal auditor – which would not be the case.

The specific objectives that the auditor must follow are:

d ISA Statement	Plain English statement
To determine whether, and to what extent, to use specific work of the internal auditors.	The external auditor needs to consider whether the work carried out by the internal auditor provides evidence that is useful to assist in forming the audit opinion.
If using the specific work of the internal auditors, to determine whether that work is adequate for the purposes of the audit.	Where internal auditors work appears to be useful, then the external auditor must review this to ensure that work can actually be relied on.

Decisions in placing reliance on internal audit

There are three key decisions that the external auditor must make before reliance can be placed on the work of the internal auditor. These decisions are:

1. can I place reliance on the internal audit department?

2. can I confirm that internal audit work will decrease my work? and

3. how do I evaluate the specific work undertaken by internal audit?

These questions and the appropriate responses are summarised below:

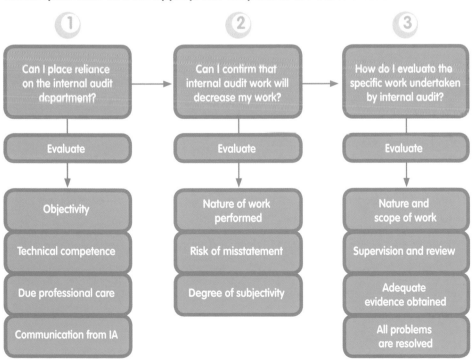

Question	Explanation
①	Here the external auditor is ensuring that the internal auditor can produce work of an acceptable standard. Effectively the external auditor is ensuring that the internal auditor follows the same standard of work as the external auditor. Therefore the internal auditor has the same standards of objectivity, technical competence and professional care that the external auditor would follow. The internal auditor should be able to talk to the external auditor directly, rather than via the directors who could "censor" any communication making it unreliable. Note that the internal auditor does not have to be qualified (although many are). Therefore the external auditor cannot simply assume that the internal auditor is following the same standards; this has to be checked again.
②	When the external auditor has decided that reliance can be placed on the work of internal audit, it is useful to ensure that the specific work will be produced. The external auditor therefore talks to the internal auditor to ensure that internal audit work does relate to the correct areas, that materiality levels are being set correctly and that work will be documented etc.
③	Finally, after the internal audit has actually carried out their work, the external auditor needs to review this work to ensure reliance can be placed on it. Again the standard expected is the same as that of the external auditor. Internal audit work must therefore be correctly planned, carried out and reviewed before reliance can be placed.

Summary

So to be clear, the external auditor:

1. evaluates the internal audit department

2. ensures their work can be relied on because it does decrease the external auditor's work, and

3. reviews the specific work performed to ensure it maintains the same standard as the external auditor.

5.14 Reliance on experts

Reliance on experts relates to situations where the auditor does not have the skills or knowledge to carry out an auditing procedure, for example valuing a building or confirming the quality and therefore value of precious gems such as diamonds. In this case, the auditor may employ an expert to provide the necessary evidence.

Overview of the ISA

ISA 620 *Using the work of an auditor's expert* explains how the auditor places reliance on an expert. As with using the work of the internal auditor, use of an expert does not decrease the auditor's responsibility for the audit opinion; although if the expert's evidence is satisfactory, the auditor can rely on it.

The ISA also refers to "management's experts". These are experts employed by the company's management (not the auditor) to provide specialist advice as management prepare the financial statements. To be clear, the auditor can evaluate the evidence produced by the management's expert in the same was as any other audit evidence. This ISA explicitly refers to auditor's experts only and how the auditor evaluates their evidence as a basis for the audit opinion.

Key things you must understand are:

1. the auditor's objectives regarding use of an expert

2. how to decide on whether an expert is needed

3. how to choose an expert, and

4. how to ensure that the expert's report is accurate.

These things are explained in the next sections.

Auditor's objectives

The main issue here is whether the auditor has the necessary knowledge or not to carry out various audit procedures. You may recall the basic ethical statement (from chapter 2) in that if an auditor does not have the skills or competence to do something then that work should not be attempted. In other words, auditors should recognise any knowledge deficiency and so look to employ an expert where necessary.

The specific objectives that the auditor must follow are quite straightforward (for a change!):

d ISA Statement	Plain English statement
To determine whether to use the work of an auditor's expert.	The auditor must decide whether an expert is needed.
If using the work of an auditor's expert, to determine whether that work is adequate for the auditor's purposes.	Evaluate the report on work from that expert to ensure that the auditor can place reliance on it.

Decisions in using an expert

There are three questions that the engagement partner must answer in using an expert:

1. Firstly, do I need an expert?

2. Secondly, how do I evaluate the skills of an expert? and

3. Thirdly, how do I evaluate the work of the expert?

These three questions with outline answers are given below:

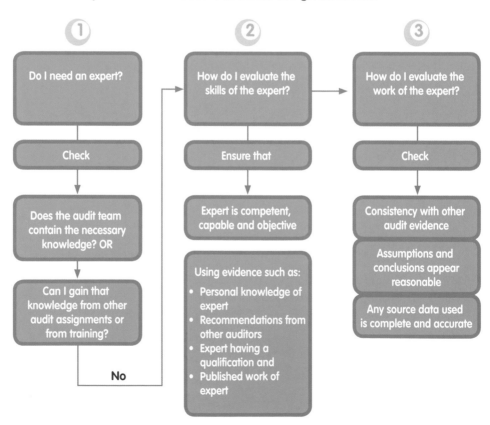

Question	Explanation
①	Sometimes knowledge can be obtained from within the audit firm; if not an expert is needed.
②	The auditor does not choose any expert; key information to obtain in making that choice is noted above.
③	When the expert presents a report, the auditor must check this is accurate. There are three tests to check accuracy listed above.

Using an expert appears straightforward? Let's check with an example.

 ## Using an expert at 27/4Books

Let's assume that the warehouse where 27/4Books store their books needs valuing this year. The auditor could guess at this figure, but a professional valuer should be able to give a more accurate figure.

The engagement partner has used a valuer before and is satisfied with their work. An appropriate contract is agreed and signed, the valuer goes away, values the building, writes the report and sends this to the partner. The value of the building is $525,000. How do we know that is correct? There are three criteria we can apply:

Criterion	Comment
Consistency with other audit evidence.	The auditor can look at the value of similar warehouses on the Internet or by reviewing estate agents adverts in newspapers. Similar warehouses should have similar values.
Assumptions and conclusions appear reasonable.	The valuer has probably noted that the warehouse appears to be in good repair (hopefully it is) although without carrying out a full structural survey. The auditor also noted this when visiting the client hence the assumption is reasonable.
Any source data used is complete and accurate.	The valuer will state the size of the warehouse, the building material used, the age of the building etc in making the valuation. The auditor can again verify that these facts are correct by looking at title deeds and the structure of the warehouse itself.

In other words, the auditor can be fairly sure that the valuer's valuation is in the correct "ballpark" or in audit terms is materially correct. It is only if similar properties had significantly different values that the auditor may be concerned and ask the valuer to justify the value chosen. Again, if the valuer could do this then the auditor may well decide to accept the valuer's report.

5.15 So where are we now?

Ready to start collecting audit evidence in practice, rather than just in theory. The next two chapters explain evidence collection in detail, starting with the Income Statement and then the Statement of Financial Position.

5.16 Summary of the summary

Finally the chapter summary:

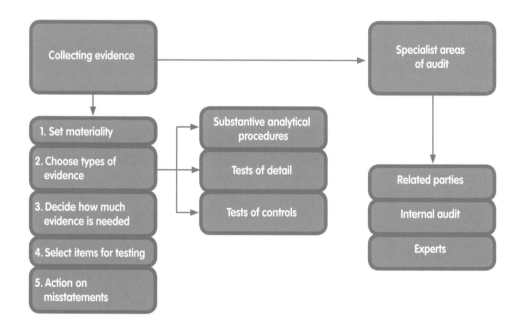

Chapter 6

The audit cycle

evidence collection 1

6.1 Introduction – what will you learn?

This chapter explains the five major transaction systems in a company and how an auditor attempts to audit those systems. I use our "client" 27/4Books to try to explain these systems and provide some (quite large) tables to break down audit work to show what does happen.

By the end of the chapter you should be seeing more into the mind of an auditor (oh dear!) and understand why auditors always ask questions. All they are really doing is ensuring that transactions have been correctly recorded in a company, as you will see.

6.2 So, what is in this chapter?

Specifically this chapter covers:

- what are the income statement audit assertions and why auditors use them
- the five main transaction cycles in a company and the control objectives for those cycles
- how the transaction cycles are audited in the context of our client 27/4Books.

To start with, here are the audit assertions.

6.3 Audit assertions

Introduction to audit assertions

Apart from having the overall objective of ensuring that financial statements show a true and fair view (see chapter 9 for audit reports on this matter), auditors have other sub-objectives. These sub-objectives are called *Assertions*. In audit terms these are statements or declarations made by the management of a company about the financial information presented to the auditor.

For example, I can assert to you that the sky is blue and the moon is made of green cheese. You could ensure that my assertions or statements are correct by, initially, looking at the sky (which hopefully is blue today?). That is, you collect evidence to ensure what I said was correct. You could also ensure that the moon is, or is not, made of green cheese by going there (quite expensive) or by using other evidence such as evidence brought back from the moon landings. This "expert" evidence will hopefully refute my assertion.

So, what are these assertions made by the directors about the financial statements? ISA 315 which explains that an auditor must *Identify and assess the risks of material misstatement through understanding the entity and its environment* contains three lists of assertions which the auditor must ensure are true. These lists are:

(i)   Assertions about clauses of Transactions (the Income Statement)

(ii)   Assertions about account balances, and

(iii)   Assertions about presentation and disclosure ((ii) and (iii) being the Statement of Financial Position).

The important list for now is that relating to the income statement; the assertions about the statement of financial position will be explained in the next chapter.

The audit assertions

d and k Regarding the income statement, the directors assert five things:

Assertion	ISA statement	Plain English statement
Occurrence	Transactions and events that have been recorded have occurred and pertain to the entity.	Sales and purchases shown in the income statement belong to the company and are real, that is they actually took place.
Completeness	All transactions and events that should have been recorded have been recorded.	All the individual transactions making up the balances in the income statement are recorded; no sales or purchases are missing.
Accuracy	Amounts and other data relating to recorded transactions and events have been recorded appropriately.	The values and any written information in the income statement are recorded at their correct amounts; no recording errors have occurred.
Cut-off	Transactions and events have been recorded in the correct accounting period.	The income statement for say the year ended 31 December 2009 only contains sales and purchases for 2009, nothing relates to 2008 or 2010.
Classification	Transactions and events have been recorded in the proper accounts.	All individual transactions are shown under the correct heading; for example, the amount stated for interest only includes interest paid and interest is not included under any other heading such as light and heat.

The auditor has to make sure that these assertions are true by obtaining audit evidence.

Remember the 5 assertions here are OCACC or "Only Competent Accountants Can Count!"

6.4 Assertions – what could go wrong?

As mentioned above, auditors check that the assertions made by the directors are correct; for example, there is completeness of recording. But, unfortunately, this is where auditors get a little strange. Rather than simply tracing transactions through an accounting system, auditors try to

- guess what could go wrong within the system
- look for controls within the system that should stop that error occurring, and finally
- test the control and/or trace transactions through a system to ensure that the control worked.

For example, in a sales system, the auditor will be thinking:

1. what is the assertion?
2. what is the audit objective relating to that assertion – so what does the assertion mean for that specific transaction type?
3. what could go wrong? Literally what could stop the assertion being true?
4. how do I ensure this error has not happened? That is the test of control or substantive procedure to confirm that the error has not occurred.

Later in this chapter we will look at the transaction systems in a company and try to answer these questions for each system.

6.5 Understanding audit assertions

This section is an introductory session to explain the rest of this chapter. Each of the transaction cycles has its own section following this introduction. Each section explains the following:

1. the general approach to auditing that cycle in terms of the audit assertions and how an auditor ensures each assertion is true

2. a diagram showing in overview how each assertion is audited

3. a detailed example from our client 27/4Books to put the theory into practice, and

4. a table showing audit procedures for transaction cycle.

But before the detail, this section explains each of the above steps. You need to read this section to understand the structure of the rest of this chapter, and then each of the transaction cycle sections in turn to understand how this introduction applies to that transaction cycle.

This is a fairly large chapter so it is worth reading through each transaction cycle individually and having a break, rather than all at once.

1 - General audit approach

The general audit approach is shown in a table. There are four columns, as shown below. The numbers in the headings relate to the four "thoughts" or questions auditors ask as already mentioned above.

1. Assertion	2. Audit objective	3. What could go wrong?	4. How do I ensure this error has not happened?
Already explained above.	This is the objective of the auditor for that assertion.	This is the error that could stop the assertion being correct or true.	This is the audit procedure which ensures that the error has not happened.

After each table, a diagram shows the sequence of activities highlighting the assertions. The activities may not be clear yet – these are explained in more detail later in the chapter using our client 27/4Books.

2 - Audit of assertions - diagram

Each diagram shows a "big picture" of how assertions for that transaction cycle are audited. Orange boxes on each diagram show the stages in the transaction cycle, moving from left to right and green shows the assertions that are being covered.

3 - Assertions – specific audit procedures

This third section explains what happens in each transaction cycle for our client 27/4Books. The systems within 27/4Books are shown both in a diagram and then explained in detail.

4 - Audit procedures

Finally, audit procedures are explained in terms of what could go wrong in each transaction cycle, and the auditor's response to those errors in terms of tests of control and substantive procedures.

The auditor's approach to each system is presented as a table. Each table has five rows, as shown below.

Activity	Explanation
What could go wrong?	This is the error that the auditor thinks could happen, e.g. incorrect quantities recorded on computer.
Why is this a problem?	This is some additional explanation to try to show why the auditor is concerned e.g. incorrect quantities recorded means subsequent documents such as invoices will also be incorrect.
Company control to prevent this	This is the control that the company has already implemented to try to stop the error happening. For example, a clerk enters order details and checks on-screen that details are correct.
Auditor – test of control	This is the actual test of control that the auditor will perform to ensure that the company control is working. For example, review computer controls and procedures including use of controls such as passwords and use of test data.
Auditor - substantive procedure	Finally, this is additional substantive testing to re-perform the activity to again confirm that the error has not happened. For example, trace order details from email or paper order onto computer system order file.

What you will need to do is read through the explanation of each system in 27/4Books and then work through the auditor's approach to that system in the table. When you have done this you will then see what specific audit procedures (tests of control and substantive procedures) are applied to each error. From the examination perspective, working through this example will provide valuable practice in determining the specific procedures necessary in your examination questions. However, every exam scenario is different so you will need to apply your knowledge to that specific scenario.

If you need to revise what are tests of controls and substantive procedures then please see chapters 4 and 5.

6.6 Transaction cycle 1: Sales

1 - General audit approach

Sales are the total value of amounts sold to customers buying goods/services from a company.

Assertion	Audit objective	What could go wrong?	How do I ensure this error has not happened?
Occurrence	All sales must relate to the company making the sale.	The sale does not belong to the company.	Working back from the recording of the sale, find the original sales order which authorised the transaction.
Completeness	All sales must be recorded.	Some sales are not recorded.	Trace individual sales all the way through an accounting system; that is sales order through to sales total in the financial statements.
Accuracy	All sales must be recorded at the correct amount in the sales day book and the correct receivables ledger/ nominal ledger accounts.	Errors are made in recording some sales.	Trace sales transactions through the system confirming the correct amount has been recorded from the order to the receivables ledger and nominal ledger.

Assertion	Audit objective	What could go wrong?	How do I ensure this error has not happened?
Cut-off	Sales must be recorded in the same accounting period as goods are despatched to the customer.	Sales are recorded in the wrong accounting period.	Ensure that the sale is recorded in the same accounting period as goods being despatched (so sales are removed from inventory and included in the Sales Day Book (SDB) in the same month).
Classification	Sales must be correctly recorded under "sales" in the financial statements.	Sales are recorded under another accounts heading such as purchases.	Trace individual sales to the sales account in the financial statements.

The assertions for this transaction cycle can also be shown as follows. Orange shows what happens to the sale and green the assertions that are being covered. To be clear, completeness and accuracy assertions are tested from the order through to the nominal ledger, while the occurrence assertion is tested from the nominal / receivables ledger back to the order document.

2 - Audit of assertions – diagram

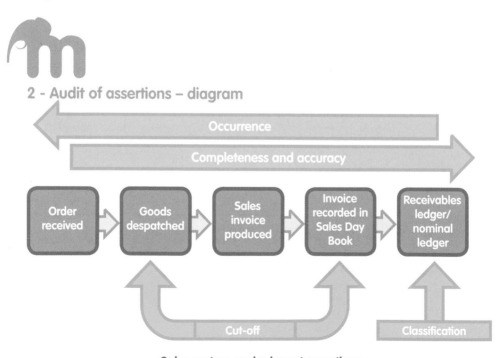

Sales system and relevant assertions

3 - Assertions – specific audit procedures

Here is the sales system in 27/4Books, followed by the auditor's approach to that system. This diagram is explained on the next page.

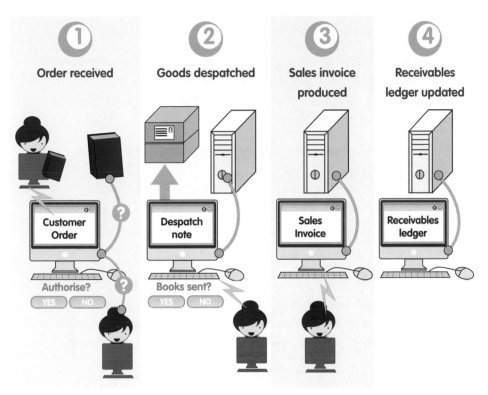

① Order received

An order is received from a customer () – probably electronically using email or Electronic Data Interchange (EDI), although sometimes in the post. A clerk enters the order information onto 27/4Books' computer system where it is stored in an order file with a unique sequential reference number being allocated to each order.

Computer checks are carried out to ensure that the required books are available in the warehouse (■) and also to ensure that the customer is real (that is they have an account at 27/4Books and that they are paying regularly for their book purchases so they are not a bad credit risk).

The order is authorised by a clerk clicking ⬤YES to the computer query after these checks have taken place.

② Goods despatched

Order information is transferred to a despatch note file on the computer and the despatch note printed out.

The books are taken from the warehouse using the despatch note to determine which books to find and then despatched () to the customer with a paper despatch note. An electronic copy of the despatch note is retained in a despatch note file on 27/4Books' computer system using the same reference number as the order.

The despatch is confirmed by a clerk clicking ⬤YES to the computer query. The computer will then send despatch confirmation electronically to the customer (in addition to the paper copy mentioned above) and start the process of updating the sales information in 27/4Books' records as explained below.

③ Sales invoice produced

A sales invoice is produced by the computer and sent electronically to the customer. The invoice is recorded in 27/4Books' computer system () initially in a sales day book – that is a list of all sales made. The invoice is allocated the same unique reference number as the order and despatch note.

④ Receivables ledger updated

The sales invoice information is used by the computer to update the receivables ledger – the individual account of each customer will be updated with the sale made so that the total amount owed by that customer to 27/4Books is known.

Finally, total sales for the day will be transferred to the nominal ledger and finally the financial statements.

4 - Audit procedures

Finally, the audit procedures for the sales cycle.

Activity	Order received	Goods despatched	Sales invoice produced / recorded	Receivables ledger updated
What could go wrong?	Incorrect books and/or incorrect quantities recorded on computer.	Incorrect books and or quantity of books sent to customer.	Invoice details incorrect e.g. quantities incorrect or wrong customer name.	Invoice not recorded in sales day book.	Wrong customer account updated with sales information.	Correct account updated but with incorrect data e.g. sales amount is incorrectly recorded.
Why is this a problem?	The customer will be sent the wrong books and may not pay for them!	The customer has been sent the wrong books and might not pay for them!	Invoice details will not agree to the books despatched so the sales figure will be incorrect.	The customer will not be recorded and sales will be understated.	When the customer pays the invoice amount will not agree to the payment received – time is wasted identifying why the error occurred.
Company control to prevent this	Clerk enters order details and checks on-screen that details are correct.	Computer transfers order information across to despatch note file.	Computer transfers despatch information across to sales invoice file / SDB reducing the risk of manual error.		Computer transfers SDB information to receivables ledger.
Auditor – test of control	Review computer controls and procedures including use of controls such as passwords and use of test data to trace transactions from order through to inclusion in the correct receivables ledger accounts.			
Auditor - substantive procedure	Trace order details from email or paper order onto computer system order file.	Trace order details from computer order file to despatch note file ensuring details agree.	Trace despatch note information to sales invoice information in SDB.	Numeric sequence test of SDB.	Trace individual sales invoice details from sales day book to receivables ledger.

A note on controls testing

There are two points to make about controls testing.

Firstly, it appears from the table above that simply because a company uses a computer, then computer controls can always be relied on. This is not the case and some transactions will always be manually traced through a system in the same way as the auditor conducts substantive procedures, as outlined above. This transaction testing will normally be carried out by internal audit.

Secondly, if this system was manual rather than computerised, then controls testing would be different.

For example:

What could go wrong?	Auditor test of manual control
Incorrect books sent to customer.	Ensure despatch note signed by despatch staff indicating agreement of despatch to original order.
Sales invoice details recorded in ledger incorrectly.	Ensure invoice signed by accounts clerk to confirm correct recording.
Incorrect receivables account updated.	As above, invoice signed.

In other words, the auditor will normally be seeking out authorisation controls. Substantive procedures would still be used to trace transactions through a system, although now of course, the books and records would be manually maintained, rather than computerised.

6.7 Credit notes

What have not been mentioned above are credit notes.

Occasionally a customer returns goods to a company, which means that a "sale" must be made in reverse; literally the customer's account is credited with the value of the goods not required.

In summary, the following activities take place:

① Goods returned

The books returned are checked to ensure they are not damaged; if damaged by the customer then a credit note will not normally be issued.

The inventory system will also be updated to show the returned books.

② Credit note issued

A credit note is issued with a copy being sent to the customer to confirm that the goods have been received. The credit note also "cancels" the sales invoice; this is no longer payable by the customer as the books have not been purchased.

③ Receivables ledger updated

The credit note information is used by the computer to update the receivables ledger – the individual account of the customer will be updated with the credit made so that the total amount owed by that customer to 27/4Books is decreased.

There is no big table showing all the errors that can take place and the audit work to ensure those errors have not occurred as this is essentially sales in reverse. However, it is something you could produce yourself for homework.

6.8 Transaction cycle 2 : Purchases

1 - General audit approach

Purchases are the total amounts obtained from suppliers of goods/services for the year.

Assertion	Audit objective	What could go wrong?	How do I ensure this error has not happened?
Occurrence	All purchases must be necessary for that particular company and actually ordered by the company.	The purchase is not a bona fide company expense.	Working back from the recording of the purchase, find the original purchase order which authorised the transaction- ensuring that the purchase is valid for that company.
Completeness	All purchases must be recorded.	Some purchases are not recorded.	Trace individual purchases all the way through an accounting system (recording of order through to financial statements) OR review supplier statements for purchases not recorded (see payables testing in the next chapter for an explanation of this procedure).
Accuracy	All purchases must be recorded at the correct amount in the purchase day book, and correct payables ledger/nominal ledger accounts.	Errors are made in recording some purchases.	Trace individual purchases through the system confirming accuracy of recording (order to PDB and the payables and nominal ledgers).
Cut-off	Purchases must be recorded in the same accounting period as goods are received from the supplier.	Purchases are recorded in the wrong accounting period.	Trace invoices in the PDB just before and after the year end to Goods Receipt Notes ensuring goods received in the same year as invoice recorded in the PDB. Where goods received pre-year end and invoice recorded post-year end, ensure purchase accrual is setup.
Classification	Purchases must be correctly recorded under "purchases" or correct expense account such as light and heat in the financial statements.	Purchases are recorded under another accounts heading such as sales.	Trace individual purchases to the expense accounts in financial statements.

The assertions for this transaction cycle can also be shown as follows. Orange shows what happens to the purchase and green the assertions that are being covered. To be clear, completeness and accuracy assertions are tested from the order through to the nominal ledger, while the occurrence assertion is tested from the nominal / payables ledger back to the order document.

2 - Audit of assertions – diagram

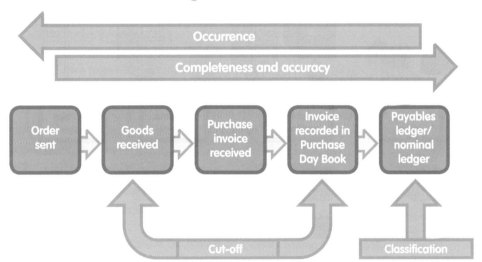

Purchases system and relevant assertions

4 - Audit procedures

Finally, the audit procedures for the purchases cycle.

Activity	Order sent	Goods received	Purchase invoice received			Payables ledger updated	
What could go wrong?	Incorrect order for books sent to supplier (e.g. order not approved).	Incorrect books and or quantity of books received from supplier.	Purchase invoice details do not match goods received details on computer.	Invoice incorrectly recorded e.g. quantities incorrect or wrong supplier name.	Invoice not recorded in purchase day book.	Wrong payable account updated with purchase information.	Correct payable account updated but with incorrect data e.g. purchase amount is incorrectly recorded.
Why is this a problem?	27/4Books will receive the wrong books and will not want to pay for them - or needs to return them.	27/4Books has been sent the wrong books and will not want to pay for them - or needs to return them.	The value of books received will be different to the value on the purchase invoice	The book purchase will not be recorded correctly either understating or overstating the purchases figure in the PDB and financial statements.	The book purchase will not be recorded understating the purchases figure in the PDB and financial statements.	The wrong supplier is paid.	The correct supplier is paid the wrong amount.
Company control to prevent this	Clerk enters order details and compares the order to the details on-screen confirming that details are correct.	Clerk enters actual goods received details and checks the details on-screen that the details are the same as the order.	Clerk agrees invoice details to goods received information before confirming invoice is correct.	Clerk confirms accurate transfer of purchase invoice details to computer by comparing paper invoice to details shown on computer screen.		Computer transfers purchase day book information to payables ledger.	
Auditor – test of control	Review computer controls and procedures including use of controls such as passwords and use of test data to trace transactions from order through to inclusion in the correct payables ledger accounts.						
Auditor – substantive procedure	Compare order from ordering department to details recorded on computer.	Trace order details from computer order file to goods received file ensuring details agree.	Trace details of goods received to the purchase invoice on the computer.	Trace details of goods received to the purchase invoice on the computer.	Same test as shown on the left or carry out a payables reconciliation on the final audit – see next chapter.	Trace individual purchase invoice details from purchase day book information to payables ledger.	

A note on controls testing

There are two points to make about controls testing.

Firstly, remember internal audit will still verify the computer controls, as already noted in the sales system above.

Secondly, if this system was manual rather than computerised, then controls testing would be different.

For example:

What could go wrong?	Auditor test of manual control
Incorrect books received from supplier.	Ensure despatch note signed by despatch staff indicating agreement of receipt to original order.
Purchase invoice details recorded in ledger incorrectly.	Ensure invoice signed by accounts clerk to confirm correct recording.
Incorrect payables account updated.	As above, invoice signed.

In other words, the auditor will normally be seeking out authorisation controls. Substantive procedures would still be used to trace transactions through a system, although now of course, the books and records would be manually maintained, rather than computerised.

6.9 Credit notes

 What have not been mentioned above are credit notes.

Occasionally a company returns goods perhaps because they were damaged in transit. In this case 27/4Books may have over-ordered from a publisher and so will return the unsold books because these are on a "sale or return" basis. This means that a "purchase" must be made in reverse, literally our purchase account is credited with the value of the books sent back.

In summary, the following activities take place:

① Goods returned

The books not required are returned to the supplier.

The inventory system will also be amended (that is the number of books decreased) to show that books have been returned.

② Credit note issued

A credit note is received back from the supplier confirming receipt of the books. The credit note also "cancels" the purchase invoice; this is no longer payable by 27/4Books as the books have not been purchased.

③ Payables ledger updated

The credit note information is used by the computer to update the payables ledger – the individual account of the payable will be updated with the credit made so that the total amount owed to that payable by 27/4Books is decreased.

Again there is no big table showing all the errors that can take place and the audit work to ensure those errors have not occurred as this is essentially purchases in reverse.

6.10 Transaction cycle 3 : Receipts

1 - General audit approach

Receipts are amounts paid by customers for items previously purchased.

Assertion	Audit objective	What could go wrong?	How do I ensure this error has not happened?
Occurrence	All receipts must relate to amounts owed to the company – that is paid by receivables for sales previously made.	The receipt does not belong to the company (Ok unlikely, but possible an invoice is paid twice).	Trace the receipt to the receivables ledger ensuring it relates to specific invoices in that receivables account.
Completeness	All receipts must be recorded.	Some receipts are not recorded.	Carry out a receivables circularisation looking for payments made by customers, but not recorded in the receivables ledger account (see chapter 7 for more details).
Accuracy	All receipts must be recorded at the correct amount and in the correct receivables ledger/ nominal ledger accounts.	Errors are made in recording some receipts.	Trace individual receipts through the system confirming accuracy of recording OR receivables circularisation as above.
Cut-off	Receipts should be recorded as soon as monies are received by company. (Note below).	Receipts are recorded in the wrong accounting period.	Trace receipts from cash book to bank statement ensure recorded in same month.
Classification	Receipts must be correctly recorded in the bank account in the financial statements.	Receipts are recorded under another accounts heading such as purchases. OK, not very likely but outside possibility.	Trace individual receipts to the bank account in the financial statements.

NOTE. Cut-off is a strange assertion with receipts. Basically receipts should be recorded as soon as the cash/cheque/internet transfer is received. The only problem with not doing this is that the bank account will be lower than expected and receivables higher than expected at the year-end. As most companies want money in the bank as soon as possible there is only a very small risk that amounts are not recorded when received. This error can only be caused by cash or cheques not being banked promptly; Internet receipts are sent straight to the company's bank account.

The assertions for this transaction cycle can also be shown as follows. Orange shows what happens to the receipt and green the assertions that are being covered. To be clear, completeness and accuracy assertions are tested from the order through to the nominal ledger, while the occurrence assertion is normally tested by ensuring that the receipt relates to a valid balance in the receivables ledger.

2 - Audit of assertions – diagram

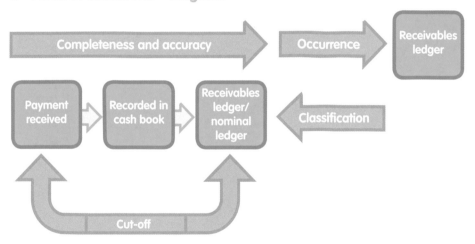

Receipts system and relevant assertions

3 - Assertions – specific audit procedures

Thirdly, receipts from our customers: note that the auditor's approach to receipts and payments is combined into one table after the section on payments.

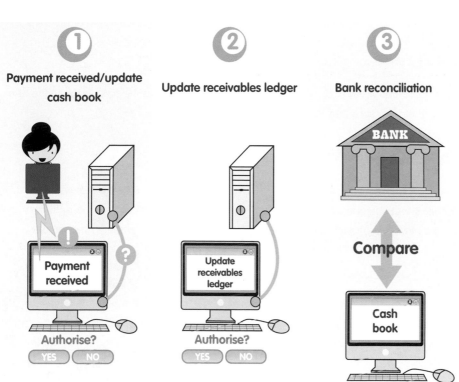

① Payment received / update cash book

A customer makes a payment to 27/4Books ( ) The payment is likely to be made by electronic banking (over the Internet). A clerk will review 27/4Books' bank statement for receipts and either transfer this information manually or copy the bank information into 27/4Books' cash book if this program can read the electronic bank information. The clerk confirms the update of the cash book by clicking (YES) in response to the computer's query.

After the transfer the clerk will compare the list of receipts in the cash book to the bank statement to ensure that all receipts have been recorded.

② Update receivables ledger

The clerk confirms by clicking (YES) to the computer query that the receivables ledger should be updated. This means that the computer will update the individual ledger accounts of each receivable with the cash book list of amounts received.

③ Bank reconciliation

A bank reconciliation will then be performed. This will agree the balance shown on the cash book in 27/4Books' accounting system with the cash balance shown on the bank statement. See chapter 7 for more information on the audit of cash/bank and bank reconciliations.

4 - Audit procedures

Audit procedures for receipts have been combined with payments to keep all "cash" transactions together in one table. See the end of the following section on payments for audit procedures on receipts.

6.11 Transaction cycle 4: Payments

1. General audit approach

Payments are amounts paid to the suppliers for goods/services supplied to the company.

Assertion	Audit objective	What could go wrong?	How do I ensure this error has not happened?
Occurrence	All payments must relate to amounts owed by the company – that is paid to payables for purchases previously made.	The payment does not belong to the company. That is something is paid for something not ordered.	Find the original purchase order which authorised the transaction.
Completeness	All payments must be recorded.	Some payments are not recorded.	Either trace payments from payment authorisation to cash book recording OR perform a bank reconciliation to identify payments made not recorded in the bank account (see chapter 7 for detail on bank reconciliations).
Accuracy	All payments must be recorded at the correct amount and in the correct payables ledger/nominal ledger accounts.	Errors are made in recording some payments.	Trace individual payments from payments listings to bank account and payables ledger confirming accuracy of recording.
Cut-off	Payments should be recorded as soon as the payment is made by the company. (Note below).	Payments are recorded in the wrong accounting period.	Trace payments in the cash book to bank statement in the same month or bank reconciliation.
Classification	Payments must be correctly recorded in the bank account in the financial statements.	Payments are recorded under another account heading such as purchases. OK, not very likely.	Trace individual payments to the bank account in the financial statements.

NOTE. Cut-off is a strange assertion with payments. Basically payment should be recorded as soon as the cash/cheque/internet transfer is raised or made. The only problem with delaying recording and making payments is that the bank account will be higher than expected and payables lower than expected at the year-end making the statement of financial position look better than it is.

The assertions for this transaction cycle can also be shown as follows. Orange shows what happens to the receipt and green the assertions that are being covered. To be clear, completeness and accuracy assertions are tested from the payment through to the nominal ledger or by carrying out a bank reconciliation, while the occurrence assertion is normally tested by ensuring that the payment relates to a valid purchase order or goods actually received.

2 - Audit of assertions – diagram

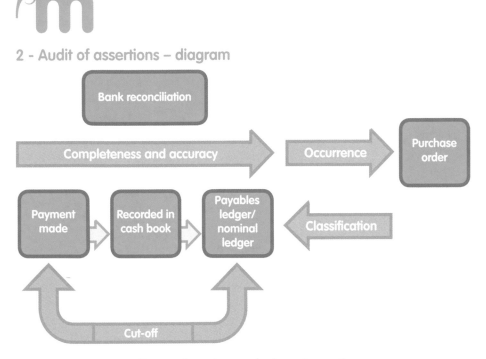

Payments system and relevant assertions

3 - Assertions – specific audit procedures

Fourthly payments to our payables.

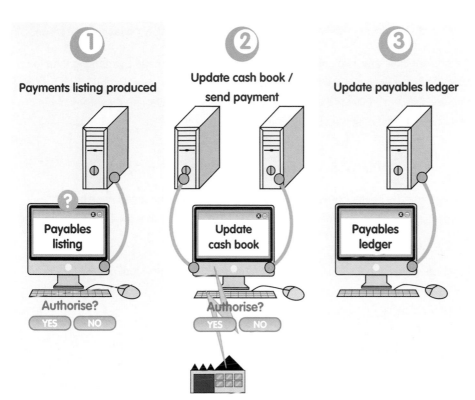

① Payments listing produced

At the end of each calendar month, the accounting programme provides a list of payables balances. This listing shows all payables with a list of the invoices due to be paid for that payable. The listing may be printed out, or simply reviewed on-screen.

A clerk identifies any invoices not to be paid and identifies these by marking them on the printout, or ticking a box on-screen by that invoice. A senior person (such as the Finance Director) reviews then signs the payment list to authorise those payments or authorises the list onscreen by clicking (YES).

② Update cash book / send payments

The data on the payments listing is transferred to the computerised cash book, normally by the clerk clicking (YES) to the computer query that the transfer should be made.

From here, payments will be made via the Internet to the individual payables (▮▮). The payment process will be the clerk entering each individual payment into 27/4Book's banking Website.

③ Update payables ledger

The clerk accesses the bank account program again and confirms update of the payables ledger by clicking (YES) to the computer query. The computer updates each payables account with the total payment being made; the balance on the account will now be any invoices not to be paid this month.

4 - Audit procedures

Finally, the audit procedures for the receipts and payments cycle.

Activity	Receipts – Payment received	Receipts – Payment recorded	Produce payments listing	Payments – Update bank account and Internet payment	Payments – Payables ledger updated
What could go wrong?	Receipt information transferred incorrectly into 27/4Books cash book (either entire payment missed or incorrectly recorded).	Receipt details used to update incorrect receivables account or details transferred incorrectly (payment amount different in receivables ledger to receipts listing).	Payments listing does not include all payables.	Payment information incorrectly transferred to the cash book (either a payment is missed or amount transferred incorrectly). / Internet payment is incorrect; either a payment is missed from the bank account or the incorrect amount recorded and then transferred.	Wrong payable account updated with payment information. / Correct payable account updated but with incorrect data e.g. payment amount is incorrectly recorded.
Why is this a problem?	Amounts received will be recorded incorrectly.	Receivable balance will be incorrect (e.g. overstated with missed payment).	Some suppliers will not be paid.	Some suppliers may not be paid, or paid the incorrect amount. / The supplier will not be paid or paid an incorrect amount.	The wrong payables account is updated so the payables ledger is incorrect. / The correct payables account is updated with the wrong amount so the payables ledger is incorrect.
Company control to prevent this	Clerk compares the bank statement with the computer list of payments received.	Computer transfers receipt information to receivables ledger.	Clerk reviews payables listing – may notice missing payables	Computer transfers amount from payments list to cash book. / Bank reconciliation carried out regularly (see chapter 7).	Computer transfers cash book payments information to payables ledger.
Auditor – test of control	Review computer controls and procedures including use of controls such as passwords and use of test data to trace transactions from order through to inclusion in the correct payables ledger accounts.				
Auditor - substantive procedure	Trace receipts details from the bank statement to the receipts listing on the computer.	Trace receipt details from receipts listing into the receivables ledger.	Normally review of supplier statements for old unpaid amounts (see payables testing: chapter 7).	Trace details from payments listing to the cash book. / Re-perform bank reconciliation.	Trace details of payments from the cash book to the individual payable accounts.

A note on controls testing

There are two points to make about controls testing.

Firstly, remember internal audit will still verify the computer controls, as already noted in the sales system above.

Secondly, if this system was manual rather than computerised, then controls testing would be different.

For example:

What could go wrong?	Auditor test of manual control
Receipt recorded incorrectly in cash book.	Ensure remittance advice signed by accounts staff indicating receipt recorded correctly.
Payment incorrectly recorded in cash book.	Cash book signed to show payments made match payables ledger balance to be paid.

In other words, the auditor will normally be seeking out authorisation controls. Substantive procedures would still be used to trace transactions through a system, although now of course, the books and records would be manually maintained, rather than computerised.

6.12 Transaction cycle 5: Salaries and wages

1 - General audit approach

Salaries and wages are amounts paid to employees for work carried out for the company.

Assertion	Audit objective	What could go wrong?	How do I ensure this error has not happened?
Occurrence	Salaries/wages are paid for work actually carried out by company employees and hours paid were actually worked.	The salary/wage does not belong to the company (that is a person is paid who is not an employee) or the work was not carried out.	Agree list of salaries/wages paid to list of valid employees in the Human Resources department / agree hours worked per payroll back to timesheets.
Completeness	All salaries/wages are recorded.	Some salary/wages are not recorded.	Trace individual salaries/wages all the way through an accounting system from recording of time worked to the salaries/wages expenses accounts in the financial statements.
Accuracy	All salaries/wages are recorded at the correct amount and in the correct nominal ledger accounts.	Errors are made in recording some salaries/wages.	Trace individual salaries/wages through the system confirming accuracy of recording.
Cut-off	Salaries/wages are recorded in the same accounting period that the work was carried out.	Salaries/wages are recorded in the wrong accounting period.	Ensure that the salary/wage is recording in the same accounting period as the work carried out by the employee.
Classification	Salaries/wages must be correctly recorded as a salary/wage expense in the financial statements.	Salaries/wages are recorded under another accounts heading such as purchases.	Trace individual salaries/wages to the salary/wages account in the financial statements.

The assertions for this transaction cycle can also be shown as follows. Orange shows what happens to the wage/salary and green the assertions that are being covered. To be clear, completeness and accuracy assertions are tested from the hours worked through to the nominal ledger, while the occurrence assertion is tested from the nominal ledger back to the hours worked document and the list of employees in the human resources department.

2 - Audit of assertions – diagram

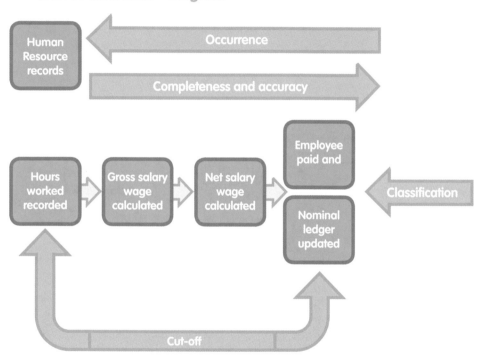

Salaries/wages system and relevant assertions

3 - Assertions – specific audit procedures

 This section is divided into two; firstly the system for salaries; this relates to staff being paid an annual fixed salary.

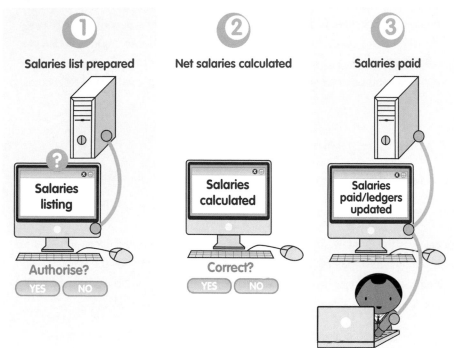

① Salaries list prepared

At the end of each month the computerised salaries programme prepares a list of all salaried employees at 27/4Books. This list is displayed on-screen and an authorised person (for example the Finance Director) confirms that the list is correct by clicking YES. The FD will specifically ensure that only valid employees are included in the list and that the salary amounts are correct. A separate record of employees may be kept for this purpose (in many companies this would be in the Human Resources department).

② Net salaries calculated

The computer system then calculates gross and net salaries for each employee.

Gross wages are simply annual salary divided by 12 (months!).

Net salary is the monthly salary less any statutory and other deductions. For example, most countries have some form of income tax which is collected by the employer and remitted to the government. Other deductions may include contributions to a pension scheme or personal saving scheme.

The FD or clerk will confirm the net salary list by clicking YES to the computer query. This authorises the salaries to be paid and tax remitted to the government.

③ Salaries paid

Following the authorisation in step 2, the computer:

transfers the net salary to the bank account of each salaried employee , and

updates the accounting system with the payments made (basically credit bank and debit the salaries expense account).

Wages

 Wages relates to staff who are paid a set amount for each hour they work.

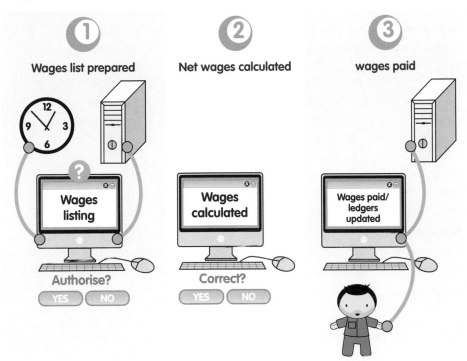

① Wages list prepared

② Net wages calculated

③ wages paid

Wages listing

Wages calculated

Wages paid/ ledgers updated

Authorise?
YES NO

Correct?
YES NO

① Wages list prepared

Wages paid for hourly paid employees are based on the actual hours worked. 27/4Books will have a system to record actual hours worked; for example, an electronic card which is passed over a reader when the employee starts and then stops work for the day. The number of hours worked is then calculated as the difference between the start and finish times.

At the end of each week or month (depending how frequently wages staff are paid) the hours worked by each worker are input to the computer system (either by a wages clerk or by transfer directly from the time recording system to the accounts computer system).

The gross wage payable by each employee is calculated by the computer (that is hours worked multiplied by hourly wage). The list is displayed on-screen and an authorised person (for example the Finance Director) confirms that the list is correct by clicking ⬤YES. The FD will specifically ensure that only valid employees are included in the list and that the wages hours and amounts are correct. A separate record of employees may be kept for this purpose (in many companies this would be in the Human Resources department).

② Net wages calculated

The computer system then calculates net wages for each employee.

Net wages is the total wage less any statutory and other deductions. For example, most countries have some form of income tax which is collected by the employer and remitted to the government. Other deductions may include contributions to a pension scheme or personal saving scheme.

The FD or clerk will confirm the net wages list by clicking ⬤YES to the computer query. This authorises the wages to be paid and tax remitted to the government.

③ Wages paid

Following the authorisation in step 2, the computer:

transfers the net wage to the bank account of each employee , and

updates the accounting system with the payments made (basically credit bank and debit the wages expense account in the nominal ledger).

4 - Audit procedures

Finally, the audit procedures for the salaries and wages cycle.

Activity	Wage calculated	Wage/salary calculation	Gross/net wages/salary calculation		
What could go wrong?	Too many or too few hours entered into computer.	Person paid not an employee of the company. Happens where an employee leaves but is not removed from the wages/salaries system.	Net salary/wage is incorrectly calculated.	Salary/wage is paid to the wrong employee. OR Salary/wage transfer not made at all.	Wrong accounts updated in computer.
Why is this a problem?	Employees will be over or under paid.	27/4Books pays an "employee" when they no longer work at the company.	Employees are paid the wrong amount of salary/wages and the incorrect salary/wage is recorded in 27/4Books records.	Employees are not paid and the salaries/wages amount is understated in 27/4Books records.	Incorrect analysis of salaries/wages in financial statements.
Company control to prevent this	Hours recorded on computer are verified as correct by clerk or authorised official.	FD reviews and authorises the list of employees prior to salaries being calculated and paid.	Computer system calculates net salary/wage. Clerk must ensure correct tax rates are entered in the computer program.	Computer system transfers net salaries/wages.	Computer system updates the accounts.
Auditor – test of control	Review computer control's and procedures including use of controls such as passwords and use of test data to trace transactions from input of hours worked through to inclusion in the correct salaries/expense account in the nominal ledger.				
Auditor - substantive procedure	If possible, the auditor will trace hours worked from the time recording system to the hours worked recorded in the computerised accounts system.	Trace a number of employees from the list of those to be paid to the authorised list maintained in the HR department. (See note below).	Re-calculate net salary/wage for a sample of employees.	Trace sample of salaries/wages paid from salaries/wages list to the bank statement confirming employee name is correct.	Trace net salary/wages expense from the salary/wages calculation to the correct ledger accounts (cash book and salaries/wages expense).

A note on controls testing

There are two points to make about controls testing.

Firstly, remember internal audit will still verify the computer controls, as already noted in the sales system above.

Secondly, if this system was manual rather than computerised, then controls testing would be different.

For example:

What could go wrong?	Auditor test of manual control
Gross or net wages / salary calculated incorrectly.	Ensure wages book signed by accounts clerk confirming wages calculation is accurate.
Wage or salary paid to wrong employee.	Wage/salary listing signed by senior official like the finance director confirming payments are for company employees and made to correct employee.

In other words, the auditor will normally be seeking out authorisation controls. Substantive procedures would still be used to trace transactions through a system, although now of course, the books and records would be manually maintained, rather than computerised.

NOTE. There may also be a separate "leavers" test where a list of employees who have left the company with the date of leaving is obtained from the HR department. The wages/salary payments for the next month are then reviewed to ensure that employees who have left are not paid in the month following the month of leaving.

6.13 So where are we now?

At the end of the most detailed chapter in this book.

You have learnt about income statement auditing (or at least now have an idea about what happens).

Treat this chapter as a reference work – when you are learning about one of the transaction cycles in your studies on auditing, go back to this chapter and refresh your memory on that cycle. I'm hoping it will enable you to understand that cycle better.

6.14 Summary of the summary

Finally the famous chapter summary (amazingly small for such a big chapter..)!

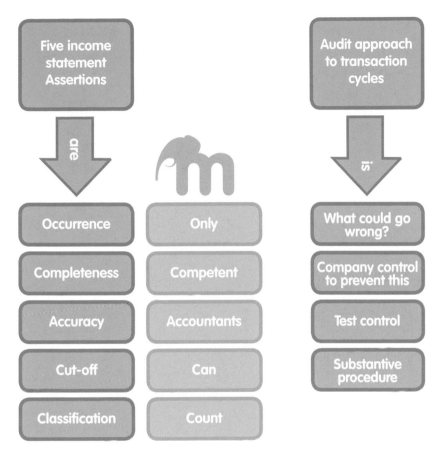

Chapter 7

The audit cycle
evidence collection 2

A student's guide to Auditing By Alan Lewin

7.1 Introduction – what will you learn?

This chapter explains the audit work on the Statement of Financial Position (sometimes abbreviated to SFP). I use our "client" 27/4Books to try and explain this audit work and provide some (quite large) tables to show what does happen.

By the end of the chapter you should understand how to audit specific SFP areas.

7.2 So, what is in this chapter?

Specifically this chapter covers:

• what the Statement of Financial Position assertions are and why auditors use them

• the audit of the main assets and liabilities on the Statement of Financial Position

• how those assets and liabilities are audited in the context of 27/4Books.

7.3 27/4Books financial statements

To (hopefully) make things a little clearer, I've given below an example Statement of Financial Position for 27/4Books. This gives an idea of the assets and liabilities in the company while the icon column gives a picture to trace into the detailed audit work later in this chapter.

27/4Books

Statement of Financial Position – 31 December 20X1

	20X1 $'000	20X0 $'000	Icon
Non-current assets	653	698	
Current assets			
Inventory	2,055	1,943	
Receivables	1,753	1,525	
Prepayments	56	50	
Cash and bank	489	506	
Total current assets	4,353	4,024	
Current liabilities			
Payables	982	886	
Accruals	101	95	
Total current liabilities	1,083	981	
Net current assets	3,270	3,043	
Total net assets	3,923	3,741	
Shareholders' funds			
Share capital	500	500	
Reserves	3,423	3,241	
Total shareholders' funds	3,923	3,741	

I'll refer back to this SFP during explanation of the audit procedures.

7.4 Standard procedures – for all Statement of Financial Position balances

Before getting into the detail of the audit of specific assets and liabilities, you need to be aware of two sets of "general" audit procedures that will always be carried out on any SFP balance. These are:

*   analytical procedures, and

*   testing the building of the total balance of that asset/liability

Both are explained below.

Analytical procedures

In overview, analytical procedures are:

d ISA statement	Plain English statement
Analytical Procedures are: "Evaluations of financial information through analysis of plausible relationships among both financial and non-financial data. Analytical procedures also encompass such investigation as is necessary of identified fluctuations or relationships that are inconsistent with other relevant information or that differ from expected values by a significant amount." (Glossary of terms – Preface to the ISAs).	The auditor will compare information about the client company including the financial statements and general knowledge of the business to make sure that changes in the amounts shown on the Income Statement and Statement of Financial Position appear "reasonable".

You will also recall that Analytical Procedures were used in chapter 5 as part of planning the audit.

ISA 520 *Analytical Procedures* provides examples of those procedures in the Application section of that standard. Example procedures given below are based on the ideas in ISA 520, along with an explanation and example taken from 27/4Books so you can see how that procedure could be used.

Example procedure	Explanation of procedure	Example
Expectations	Over the course of an audit, the auditor builds up knowledge about a client. The auditor compares this "knowledge" to the assets and liabilities in the Statement of Financial Position.	The directors of 27/4Books have stated that the company has had a "good year" – we would have expected sales to increase.
Last year's figures	The balances on the Statement of Financial Position and Income Statement are compared to last year. The auditor will have some idea of what the balance should be from knowledge of the client already gained on the audit. Any significant difference is investigated and reasons obtained for the discrepancy.	If sales have increased, then receivables will normally have increased by a similar amount. If receivables have increased by say 50% compared to sales of only 20%, then receivables appear to be high and additional audit procedures may be carried out to confirm that the balance is accurate.
Review of individual balances	The individual items making up the balance are compared to the same list from last year. Any significant differences are investigated and reasons obtained for the change.	Audit work can focus on new items with high balances (e.g. new receivables) or old items with zero balances (e.g. receivables with no amount owed to 27/4Books).
Real world	The auditor's knowledge of the industry that the client company is in.	The auditor may be aware that book distribution companies tend to have set percentage of sales as their receivables balance – 27/4Books should have a similar percentage.
Ratio analysis	The auditor calculates key ratios from the company's financial statements and obtains reasons for changes in those ratios where necessary.	Current assets ratio in 27/4Books is 20X1 : 4.01 20X0 : 4.10 The change here is quite small so the auditor is unlikely to require any detailed explanation.

Remember Analytical Procedures can always be used when auditing a SFP asset/liability.

Build up of total / transfer to financial statements

The second standard procedure on most SFP balances is to confirm that the totals on the SFP actually consist of valid individual items.

In other words, the auditor is starting to ensure that the total balance is valid; firstly by ensuring that the total is made up from valid items and then later that each item is represented by other evidence.

For example, the receivables balance will be agreed to a list of receivables and then in more detailed audit testing, a sample of receivables balances will be tested to ensure they represent "real" receivables, that is receivables actually belonging to the company. This more detailed testing is explained in the sections of this chapter dealing with each individual asset/liability.

The procedures for ensuring that a balance on the SFP is actually made up from a list of individual items are shown below:

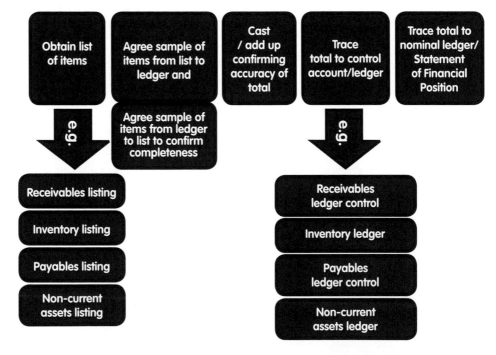

These procedures will always be carried out for SFP items so if an auditing question asks for relevant procedures on say "receivables" then repeating the above steps using the receivables listing and receivables ledger control as relevant examples will obtain credit in the answer.

7.5 Audit assertions – statement of financial position

As in chapter 6 on the income statement, this chapter explains the relevant audit assertions. However, this time the assertions are relevant to the Statement of Financial Position, that "snapshot" of the company at the end of the year showing all the assets and liabilities of the company.

d and **k** ISA 315 contains list of assertions regarding these assets and liabilities. These are the things that directors assert to be true about the assets and liabilities. The directors assert four things:

Assertion	ISA statement	Plain English statement
Existence	Assets, liabilities, and equity interests exist.	Literally if something is shown on the statement of financial position then that thing, whatever it is, does exist and is not fictitious.
Rights and obligations	The entity holds or controls the rights to assets, and liabilities are the obligations of the entity.	The assets and liabilities actually belong to the company and therefore should be on the statement of financial position. Remember Rights relates to assets and Obligations refers to liabilities.
Completeness	All assets, liabilities and equity interests that should have been recorded have been recorded.	There is nothing missing from the statement of financial position; the directors have not hidden any assets or liabilities.
Valuation and allocation	Assets, liabilities, and equity interests are included in the financial statements at appropriate amounts and any resulting valuation or allocation adjustments are appropriately recorded.	Assets and liabilities are shown at the correct value – in this case the value being determined by appropriate accounting standards.

You can remember the assertion names quite easily if you really really want to: the first letters can be re-arranged to give the mnemonic CRAVE.

Completeness

Rights

Allocation

Valuation

Existence

Ok – rights relates to assets so you need to remember obligations also for liabilities. Also, I've split the valuation and allocation assertion into two – this is helpful because it reminds you that financial statement allocation/presentation must also audited for assets/liabilities (see the next section for the disclosure assertions). Apart from this I hope you'll find this a useful memory jogger.

I've kept the order of assertions the same as in the ISA 315 in the individual sections below to match with the ISA. However, CRAVE will elicit the assertions and examination questions don't require the assertions in order so you can think of them in this order.

7.6 Audit assertions – presentation and disclosure

The final list of assertions relates to the presentation and disclosure of information in the financial statements as a whole; in other words the Income Statement, the Statement of Financial Position and any other supporting notes and information contained in the financial statements.

To be clear:

- assertions about classes of transactions (covered in chapter 6) deals with the Income Statement

- assertions about balances deals with the Statement of Financial Position, and

- assertions about presentation deals with how the income and expenditure, assets and liabilities are actually disclosed.

The assertions about presentation and disclosure are shown in the table below.

Assertion	ISA statement	Plain English statement
Occurrence and rights and obligations	Disclosed events, transactions, and other matters have occurred and pertain to the entity.	All the items referred to in the financial statements are real and do belong to the company.
Completeness	All disclosures that should have been included in the financial statements have been included.	The financial statements are complete; no information has been missed.
Classification and understandability	Financial information is appropriately presented and described, and disclosures are clearly expressed.	The financial statements contain sufficient information to ensure that the user can understand what has happened to the company during the last year.
Accuracy and valuation	Financial and other information are disclosed fairly and at appropriate amounts.	The amounts shown are included as close as possible to their correct amounts.

These assertions are not mentioned directly in this chapter. The key term Allocation in CRAVE above reminds you that presentation is also important. In overall terms we are simply ensuring that the financial statements are complete and do provide all the information that the user needs to understand those statements.

7.7 Introduction to auditing the Statement of Financial Position

This is important – please read before any of the sections on specific audit work!

As mentioned above, this chapter takes you through the audit of the assets and liabilities on the Statement of Financial Position (or SFP for short). I've tried to use a common format for each section to make the audit work easier to follow and provide consistency for the chapter.

The audit of each SFP area has the following sections.

Section	Explanation
1. What are they?	A brief statement about what the asset or liability is.
2. Relevance to 27/4Books	An explanation of that asset/liability for our client 27/4Books.
3. Analytical procedures	An example of the analytical procedures that could be used for this section of SFP audit testing.
4. Assertions relating to..	Each of the SFP assertions is explained in the context of the asset/liability and a summary of the main audit procedures to be carried out mentioned. This information is presented in a table as shown below:

Assertion	Audit objective	What could go wrong?	How do I ensure this error has not happened?	Audit procedure	Why does this proce-dure work?
Literally the assertion to be tested.	What the auditor is trying to prove in relation to that assertion.	The error if the assertion is shown to be false.	The audit approach to testing the assertion.	Specific audit procedures relevant to the asset or liability.	An explanation of why that audit procedure is used.

Following this table, the main audit procedures relating to that asset or liability are explained. Each procedure has a table like the one below to explain the procedure and detail which assertions are covered by that procedure.

What is this?	Assertions covered	Explanation of assertion
Explanation of the procedure.	Which assertion is being tested.	How or why that audit procedure is used.

The assertions covered column is colour coded to show how effective the procedure is:

Assertion	Usefulness of procedure
	Procedure is very effective.
	Procedure is partly effective.
	Procedure has limited value and would not be used to test that assertion.

Auditing individual assets or liabilities

To be clear, if you have an examination question regarding the audit of an asset or liability, then the three "sets" of procedures you will always use are:

1. analytical procedures – as mentioned above with a summary for each asset/liability below

2. build up of the total of that asset or liability – as mentioned above –, and

3. the specific procedures relating to that asset or liability – as explained below.

In other words, please don't forget steps 1 and 2 above; they will get you marks in the examination.

7.8 Receivables

1 - What are they?

Receivables are the total amounts due from customers buying goods/services from a company on credit

 ## 2 - Relevance to 27/4Books

When 27/4Books sell books to customers, those books are sold on "credit"; the books are despatched, then a sales invoice is raised with the payment for those books being received from the customer some time after the sale. Normally this time period is between one and two months, although this can be longer especially where the customer is experiencing financial difficulties.

For our client, we need to make sure that receivables are valued correctly (there are no bad receivables – that is customers who will not pay their outstanding invoices), and that the receivables balance is complete and those receivables actually exist. The receivables balance is $1,753,000 this year which is a material amount, so audit testing is required to ensure that the figure is correctly stated in the financial statements.

3 - Analytical procedures

These are example procedures for 27/4Books with a little "poetic licence" regarding the relevance to the company for example the point about the directors expecting a fairly good year to make the procedures appear "real"!

Example procedure	Relevance to 27/4Books
Expectations	The directors stated that 27/4Books had a fairly good year and budgets for the year showed a 12% increase in receivables; 15% is therefore in line with expectations.
Last year's figures	Receivables have increased by 15% ($1,525k to $1,753k) compared to sales increase of just over 15% ($9,557k to $11,023k) so this change is reasonable.
Review of individual balances	Individual balances are not given for this example, but the auditor would normally investigate: • new receivables with large balances • old receivables with small or zero balances • negative balances • receivables that have not paid within say three months of the SFP date • a random sample of the remaining balances.
Real world	Overall sales in the book industry appear to be increasing as more people read books that have become films.

4 - Assertions relating to receivables

The following table provides a summary of the audit approach to receivables. The key audit procedures of the "receivables circularisation" and "bad debt review" are explained after the table.

Assertion	Audit objective	What could go wrong?	How do I ensure this error has not happened?	Audit procedure	Why does this procedure work?
Existence	The receivable is "real" that is it does exist.	The receivable does not exist; sales and receivables are over-stated.	Obtain evidence directly from the receivable to prove that they are real.	Receivables circularisation.	Obtaining a letter or similar communication from the receivable is direct evidence of existence. This is a good evidence source because it is from a third party and is written.
Rights and obligations	The receivable belongs to the company – that is the amount shown is due to 27/4Books.	The receivable amount does not belong to 27/4Books.	Obtain evidence directly from the receivable which confirms that the debt is owed to 27/4Books.	Receivables circularisation.	The letter from the receivable is direct evidence that the amount is owed to 27/4Books.
Completeness	All receivables balances are complete; that is receivables are not under-stated.	Receivables are omitted from the financial statements.	Obtain evidence from sales invoice to ensure completeness of all sales in the receivables accounts.	In transaction testing, ensure that all sales invoices have been recorded in the correct receivables accounts.	Obtaining third party evidence does not confirm completeness – people don't tend to mention amounts due unless asked.
Valuation and allocation	The amount shown for receivables is correct – that is receivables are not over-stated (and remember correctly presented/disclosed).	Receivables do not pay the amount due; in other words they are delinquent – this is a bad debt.	Obtain evidence showing either payment being received from the receivable or confirmation that the debt will be paid.	Review payments after the year-end. Bad debt review. Receivables circularisation.	Receiving actual payment confirms that the debt will be paid. Bad debt review shows potential bad debts. A circularisation only confirms the amount due, not necessarily that it will be paid.

Audit procedures relating to receivables

The important audit procedures relating to receivables are:

- receivables circularisation, and
- bad debt review.

Although there are other procedures that can be used, these are the most important regarding examination preparation and provide the most coverage of audit assertions.

Receivables circularisation

What is this?	Assertions covered	Explanation of assertion
Sending letters to individual receivables to confirm their balance on the receivables ledger. ISA505 provides guidance on the audit procedures relating to this letter.	Existence	The receivable writes back to the auditor attaching evidence of that receivable e.g. headed notepaper or an official stamp.
	Rights and obligations	The receivable confirms that the debt is due to 27/4Books.
	Completeness	If the receivable does not receive an invoice from 27/4Books then it will not be recorded – the balance will be understated. Remember completeness is tested during transaction testing.
	Valuation and allocation	The receivable confirms that the debt is payable to 27/4Books – that is the balance is not overstated by 27/4Books recording invoices twice or in the wrong receivables account. However, the receivable does not necessarily confirm that the debt will be paid - the balance could still be disputed or the receivable go out of business. In this case the receivable will be overstated.

How to carry out the circularisation

Here are the six stages of performing a receivables circularisation.

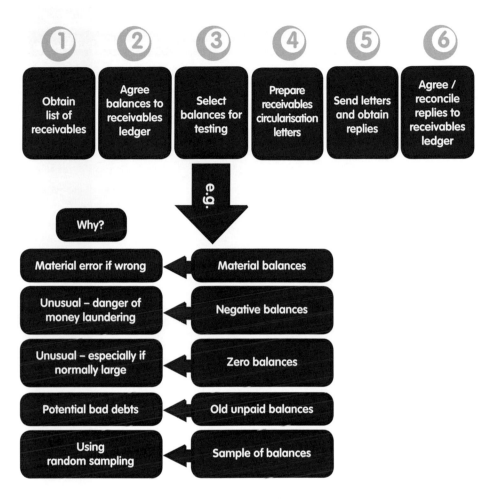

While the stages may appear logical there are a few strange points you need to be aware of:

Stage	Point
4	The letter has the balance owed to the receivable on it. The client signs the letter but the auditor will post it – to ensure that the client does not amend details after signing.
5	Replies are sent direct to the auditor – not the client – to ensure again that the client does not amend replies after receipt.
6	Sometimes the receivable cannot agree the balance due to 27/4Books. Additional receivables testing is noted below.

What happens if the receivable cannot agree the balance due or will not reply?

In these situations the auditor will need to carry out additional work.

Problem	Why is this a problem	Alternative audit work
1. Receivable does not reply.	Receivable may not exist.	Confirm payment from receivable after the year end by seeing the payment on the bank statement.
2. Receivable replies – balance is higher than they expected.	Normally means the receivable has made a payment recently not yet received by our client.	Confirm payment received after the end of the year by seeing payment on bank statement.
3. Receivable replies – balance is lower than they expected.	Normally means that an invoice has been sent to the receivable but hasn't arrived yet.	Confirm invoice is recorded in the sales day book and ledger before the end of the year.

Bad debt review

What is this?	Assertions covered	Explanation of assertion
Reviewing the aged receivables analysis some time after the year end to identify receivables with old unpaid balances which were payable at the year-end.	Existence	An old balance does not confirm existence – if anything it could indicate that the receivable does not exist as the amount has not been paid!
	Rights and obligations	There is no third party evidence to confirm the debt is due to 27/4Books.
	Completeness	If the receivable does not receive an invoice from 27/4Books then it will not be recorded – the balance will be understated. Remember completeness is tested during transaction testing.
	Valuation and allocation	The procedure confirms that some debts are old and unpaid. A bad debt provision may therefore be required with appropriate adjustments being made in the financial statements.

How to carry out the bad debt review

Here are the five stages to performing a bad debt review.

① Obtain list of receivables one month or more after year end

② Ensure that the list is "aged"

③ Identify receivables with balances more than say 3 months old

④ Discuss with the directors whether provision is required for non payment

⑤ Agree provision amount and confirm adjustment in financial statements

Stage	Point
2	"Aged" means that the receivables balance is broken down to show the month that individual invoices were sent to a receivable. Older, unpaid invoices can then be seen – the older the unpaid invoice then the more likely a bad debt will occur – that is the receivable cannot pay the balance due.
4	The discussion with directors is really the auditor asking for the directors' opinion as to why the receivable has not paid. Any disagreement will be noted by the auditor and if material the auditor may qualify the audit report (see chapter 9).
5	As you (hopefully) know this is Debit the Income Statement and Credit the receivables balance on the Statement of Financial Position.

7.9 A note on prepayments testing

1 - What are they?

Prepayments are amounts which have been paid in advance of goods or services being received, for example telephone line rental paid in advance. The most common examples are rent paid in advance and insurance premiums. Prepayments are normally a relatively small balance on the financial statements of a company which means audit work is limited.

 ### 2 - Relevance to 27/4Books

Prepayments in 27/4Books are simply insurance premiums paid in advance and amounts for telephone / Internet line rentals.

Only minimal audit work will be required because the balance is quite small.

3 - Analytical review

This procedure will normally be limited to:

Example procedure	Relevance to 27/4Books
Review of individual balances	Comparing prepayments balances this year to last year. Any changes should be in line with expectations e.g. if telephone rental charges have increased by say 5% then the prepayment should also be 5% higher.

4 - Basic audit work on prepayments

Stage	Point
②	Any significant change will be investigated by asking client staff/directors for an explanation.
③	Supporting documentation means the relevant invoice. For example, the insurance prepayment will be agreed to the insurance invoice and the prepayment amount calculated from this. So insurance paid in October for the year will be nine months prepaid at the year end (27/4Books year end being December).

7.10 Inventory

1 - What is this?

Inventory is those raw materials, work in progress and finished goods on a company's premises awaiting sale to customers. ISA 501 gives information on attendance at inventory counts and is explained later in this section

 2 - Relevance to 27/4Books

27/4Books maintains inventory ready to sell to customers who require the books. The book inventory itself is obtained from other suppliers. So to state the obvious, 27/4Books has purchased the inventory to hopefully sell on to its customers at a profit – sales price being higher than purchase price. At the year end, the inventory is an asset of 27/4Books. It must therefore be counted and included in the financial statements at an appropriate valuation.

For our client, we need to make sure that the inventory does exist and that all inventory is included in the financial statements at the correct valuation. Inventory is definitely material, at $2,055,000 it is just under half of the total asset value, so it must be audited!

3 - Analytical procedures

Example procedure	Relevance to 27/4Books
Expectations	The directors stated that 27/4Books had a fairly good year and budgets for the year showed a 10% increase in inventory; the actual increase of 6% (see below) is therefore in line with expectations.
Last year's figures	Inventory has increased by 6% ($1,943k to $2,055k) compared to sales increase of just over 15% ($9,557k to $11,023k) so this change is probably reasonable. Cost of sales did increase by 27% ($6,217k to $7,923k) indicating more purchases overall – but inventory appears to be managed well, that is not increasing too quickly.
Review of individual balances	Individual balances are not given for this example, but the auditor would normally investigate: • new inventory with large balances • inventory with few or zero sales in the last few months (possible old inventory requiring provision) • a random sample of the remaining balances (at the inventory count – see below).
Real world	Overall sales in the book industry appear to be increasing as more people read books that have become films. As with receivables this indicates that more inventory should be present in 27/4Books.

4 - Assertions relating to inventory

The table below provides a summary of the audit approach to inventory. The key audit procedures of the "attendance at inventory count" and "inventory valuation" are explained after the table.

Assertion	Audit objective	What could go wrong?	How do I ensure this error has not happened?	Audit procedure	Why does this procedure work?
Existence	The inventory is "real", that is it does exist.	Inventory may have been stolen.	See the inventory.	Attendance at inventory count.	The auditor actually sees the inventory; evidence obtained directly by the auditor being of a high quality.
Rights and obligations	The inventory belongs to the company.	27/4Books may be holding inventory for another company.	Ensure that the inventory is paid for after the end of the year.	Going concern review.	As long as the company is a going concern (see chapter 8) then inventory will be paid for so rights and obligations are not a major audit problem.
Completeness	Inventory is complete; that is there is no inventory not included in the total.	27/4Books may have inventory in another location omitted from the total.	See the inventory and confirm recording in inventory records of the company.	Attendance at inventory count.	The auditor confirms physical inventory to the inventory records in the company.
Valuation and allocation	The amount shown for inventory is correct – that is inventory is not over-stated or under-stated.	27/4Books may be holding old or damaged inventory.	Observe the condition of the inventory.	Attendance at inventory count.	The actual condition of the inventory can be seen on the inventory count and old items noted to ensure valuation is correct.
			Discuss inventory valuation with management.	Valuation testing in accordance with accounting standards.	Discussion with directors tries to ensure compliance with accounting standards.

Inventory testing

There are two main audit procedures regarding inventory

1. attendance at the inventory count, and

2. valuation testing.

Attendance at inventory count

What is this?	Assertions covered	Explanation of assertion
Attending the client's premises to ensure that inventory counting is carried out correctly.	Existence	Items are traced from the count sheets to the physical inventory to confirm inventory exists.
	Rights and obligations	The fact that the inventory is on the client's premises suggests that the client owns it; although better evidence is seeing the purchase invoice as this shows the inventory was sold to the client.
	Completeness	Inventory is traced from the physical inventory to the count sheets confirming that recording of inventory is complete.
	Valuation and allocation	The inventory count is a good place to see the actual condition of the inventory – damaged or obsolete inventory will need to be provided against. Other valuation will be carried out on the final audit - see valuation testing below.

NOTE. The assertion cut-off is normally included on an audit as part of inventory testing, even though this is an Income Statement assertion. That is why you will find cut-off testing mentioned below in audit work during the inventory count.

Auditing the inventory count

There is an auditing standard on attendance at an inventory count (ISA 501). The diagram below summarises the main sections of that standard.

As you will see, there are three main elements of the inventory count:

Before the inventory count | **During the inventory count** | **After the inventory count**

Audit work

Before	During	After
Review prior year working papers to find any problems encountered last year	Observe the count to ensure client procedures are being followed	Follow up damaged inventory information to ensure inventory valuation is correct
Review client's count instructions to ensure count will be carried out accurately	Test count sheets to inventory to confirm inventory exists	Follow up cut-off information to ensure no cut-off errors
Identify material inventory locations to send staff to correct addresses!	Test count inventory to sheets to confirm inventory is completely recorded	Ensure inventory records updated to show the actual inventory balances
Book the staff to attend and monitor the inventory count	Review condition of inventory to follow up after count for possible inventory provision	
	Obtain cut-off information (last goods receipt and goods despatch note numbers) to confirm accuracy of cut-off	
	Reach a conclusion regarding the completeness and accuracy of the inventory count	

Summary of inventory counting:

Stage	Point
1	Before the inventory count the main task of the auditor is to ensure that the count can be carried out accurately. That is why the count instructions are obtained and reviewed.
2	During the count, the main task of the auditor is to confirm the completeness and accuracy of the count itself. Attendance at inventory count is really a test of control – ensuring that the client's inventory counting system is working.
3	After the count, the auditor follows up the information obtained during the count.

Difficulties with inventory counts

Counting inventory has a few unique problems as shown below. Remember, the auditor must make every effort to obtain sufficient evidence of the existence and completeness of inventory. It is only in very rare situations that the auditor will decide that sufficient evidence cannot be obtained.

Problem	Why is this a problem?	Effect on audit work
1. The client maintains a perpetual inventory system.	The client keeps inventory records which always show the current balance of inventory (normally using a computer system). Inventory balances can be determined either by counting inventory or from the perpetual inventory records. There is no need for the client to count inventory at the year-end (inventory balances are taken from the perpetual inventory system) – or therefore the auditor to attend the inventory count.	The auditor will check the accuracy of the perpetual inventory system before the year end – performing test counts from the system to inventory and inventory back to the system. This confirms the existence and completeness of inventory.
2. The auditor cannot attend the inventory count.	There will not be sufficient audit evidence to confirm completeness and existence of inventory. The auditor may not be able to attend the count due to danger to the auditor (e.g. counting explosives!).	The auditor may seek other evidence (e.g. sales invoices for inventory after the year-end). However, this evidence is unlikely to be sufficient; therefore a modification of the audit report will be required (see chapter 9).
3. Inventory is located at a third party.	In some situations inventory is delivered to customers on a "sale or return" basis – the inventory belongs to the supplying company until it is either sold – or returned being unsold.	Alternative evidence on the existence of the inventory is needed. The auditor can rely on a statement from the auditor of the customer or a letter from the customer confirming that the inventory is on their premises.

Inventory valuation

Inventory valuation testing covers the assertion of – well – valuation. The auditor must ensure that inventory is valued in accordance with accounting standards. Hopefully you remember from your accounting studies that inventory must be valued at the lower of cost and Net Realisable Value -- per IAS 2.

So, here's a summary of the valuation method along with the audit evidence will collect to confirm that the valuation is accurate.

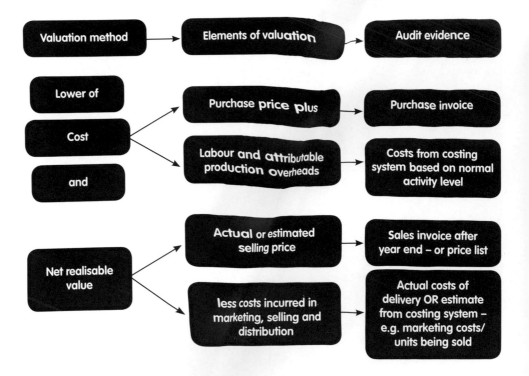

7.11 Payables

1 - What are they?

Payables represent the amount owed by a company to suppliers of goods and services.

 ### 2 - Relevance to 27/4Books

Payables are the companies that 27/4Books buys its books and services from. Books are purchased on credit – that is 27/4Books receives the books purchased and then pays for them a month or two later. The payables amount is therefore the books and services that 27/4Books has not yet paid for.

For our client, the main thing we need to make sure of is that the payables balance is complete – or the liability shown in 27/4Books will be understated. The payables balance is $982,000 – which is material so audit work is needed.

3 - Analytical procedures

Example procedure	Relevance to 27/4Books
Expectations	The directors stated that 27/4Books had a fairly good year and budgets for the year showed a 17% increase in payables; the actual increase of 11% (see below) is therefore in line with expectations and may indicate 27/4Books is paying payables earlier than necessary or that some payables are missing.
Last year's figures	Payables have increased by 11% ($886k to $982k) compared to cost of sales increase of just over 27% ($6,217k to $7,923k) so this change indicates 27/4Books ensuring that payables are paid promptly. The payables days ratio could also be calculated here to ensure payables balance appeared reasonable.
Review of individual balances	Individual balances are not given for this example, but the auditor would normally investigate: • new payables with large balances • old payables with small or zero balances • negative balances • payables that have not been paid within say three months of the SFP date • a random sample of the remaining balances.
Real world	Overall sales in the book industry appear to be increasing as more people read books that have become films. This means that purchases and therefore payables will also be increasing.

4 - Assertions relating to payables

The table below provides a summary of the audit approach to payables. The key audit procedures of the "payables statement reconciliation" and "after date payments" are explained after the table.

Assertion	Audit objective	What could go wrong?	How do I ensure this error has not happened?	Audit procedure	Why does this procedure work?
Existence	The payable is "real", that is it does exist.	Payables have been included to overstate the payables balance.	Ensure that the payables amounts are agreed to some evidence from that payable such as the purchase invoice.	Trace payables to original purchase invoices and/or orders OR payables statement.	Some third party evidence regarding the payable has been checked; third party evidence being a reliable source.
Rights and obligations	The payable belongs to the company.	27/4Books has included payables that do not belong to it.	Ensure that the payables amounts are agreed to some evidence from that payable and this is addressed to 27/4Books.	Payables statement reconciliation.	The payable confirms that the debt is due from the company – effectively confirming that the amount has to be paid to that payable.
Completeness	All payable balances are complete; that is payables are not under-stated.	Invoices near the year end have not been entered into 27/4Books' system.	Difficult as attempting to audit something that is not there (the invoice is missing) and this may also result in understating expenses - which management may want to do.	Payables statement reconciliation. Review of after date payments.	The statement shows all amounts due to the payable – if any invoices have not been recorded in the company then these will still appear on the payables statement. The omission will therefore be identified.
Valuation and allocation	The amount shown for payables is correct – that is payables are not over-stated.	The payables list has been added up incorrectly.	This error is unlikely to occur – a company will not normally overstate payables (and therefore purchases) as this decreases profit.	Payables statement reconciliation.	If payables are overstated in the company books, the invoices to which the overstatements relate will not appear on the supplier statement. The overstatement will therefore be identified.

Audit procedures for payables

The important audit procedures relating to payables are:

1. Payables statement reconciliation, and
2. After date payment review.

Although there are other procedures that can be used, these are the most important regarding examination preparation and provide the most coverage of audit assertions.

Payables statement reconciliation

What is this?	Assertions covered	Explanation of assertion
Confirming the balance due from a payable to independent evidence of that debt – in this case a document from the payable (statement) showing amounts due to that payable. ISA505 provides guidance on the audit procedures relating to this letter.	Existence	The statement from the payable is independent third party evidence confirming that the payable does exist.
	Rights and obligations	The statement confirms that the amount is due to the payable.
	Completeness	If 27/4Books has failed to record an invoice then that invoice will still appear on the payable statement – completeness of recording of invoices can therefore confirmed.
	Valuation and allocation	Valuation may not be confirmed – if 27/4Books has a dispute with a payable (for example books received were damaged and need to be returned) the payable balance may not be decreased until the payable confirms receipt of those books and confirms they were damaged.

How to carry out the payables statement reconciliation

Here are the six stages of the payables statement reconciliation.

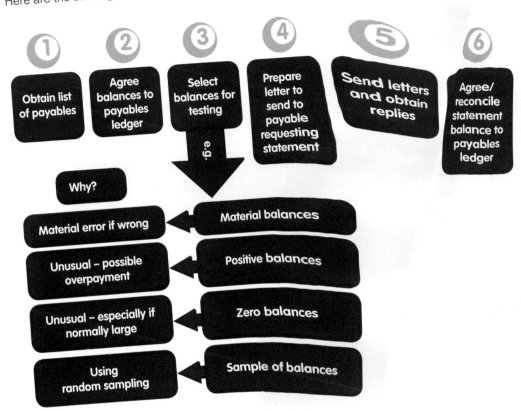

While the stages may appear logical there are a few strange points you need to be aware of:

Stage	Point
④ and ⑤	Note these stages will only be carried out where suppliers' statements are not already available at 27/4Books. Most audit clients realise auditors need suppliers statements and keep these ready for auditor use. Although there is a risk that the client has forged the statements, most will be on the supplier's headed paper decreasing this possibility.
④	The letter simply requests a statement; no balance is shown. This is because the important assertion being tested is understatement – the auditor does not want the payable to look at a balance quickly and confirm it is correct – when it may in fact be understated.
⑤	Replies are sent direct to the auditor – not the client – to ensure that the client does not amend replies after receipt. Note the auditor may also accept payables statements kept by the client rather than obtain the statement directly from the payable.
⑥	Sometimes the payables statement will not agree the balance due to 27/4Books. Additional testing is noted below.

What happens if the payables statement cannot be obtained or the statement balance does not agree to the payables ledger account?

In these situations the auditor will need to carry out additional work.

Problem	Why is this a problem?	Effect on audit work
1. Payable statement cannot be obtained.	Auditor cannot check that payable for the completeness assertion – invoices omitted from 27/4Book's ledger.	Review invoices received after the year end to see if they relate to books received before the year end - if they do then ensure an accrual has been included in the financial statements for this amount.
2. Payables statement balance is higher than the balance on the payables ledger account.	May mean that an invoice has not been recorded in 27/4Books accounts.	Trace any invoices not recorded to the invoice accruals list (see below) or ask client why the invoice is not recorded.
	May also mean that a payment from 27/4Books has not yet reached the payable.	Confirm that the payment has been recorded as received by the payable on their next statement (or at least agree payment to cash book pre-year end).

Note it is unlikely that a statement balance will be lower than that shown in 27/4Books ledger – this would mean that the payable was confirming amounts due which are less than 27/4Books had recorded. However, a lower balance is possible where 27/4Books has posted a purchase invoice to the wrong payables ledger account – effectively overstating that balance, or similarly posted a payment to that payable to a different account – again making the balance overstated.

Review of after date payments

What is this?	Assertions covered	Explanation of assertion
A review of payments made after the end of the year to try and identify any payments that relate to the previous year and therefore need an accrual setting up where necessary - that is the accrual had been missed by 27/4Books.	Existence	The review will only relate to existence where appropriate third party evidence is identified (e.g. a purchase invoice from a supplier).
	Rights and obligations	As above. Obtaining appropriate third party evidence will show that 27/4Books has an obligation to pay that third party.
	Completeness	The test is specifically attempting to ensure completeness of liabilities in the financial statements.
	Valuation and allocation	Identifying a payment does help ensure correct valuation.

How to carry out a review of after date payments

The stages to carry out a review of after date payments are:

① Obtain the cash book for about two months after the year end	② Review the cash book for large and/or unusual payments	③ Obtain supporting documentation for the payment (e.g. Invoice or voucher)	④ Where the payment relates to the prior year, ensure the relevant invoice is included in accruals listing where necessary

Stage	Point
①	This may be in paper or electronic format.
②	The auditor will need to use skill and judgement here to determine what is "unusual".
③	Supporting evidence should show what the payment was for.
④	If a payment relates to last year, then it must be included in last year's accounts. This will mean including the amount in accruals (on the Statement of Financial Position) and then the relevant expense account (on the Income Statement).

7.12 A note on accruals testing

1 - What are they?

Accruals are amounts which are payable to third parties at the
end of the year. Accruals normally relate to services supplied
which are invoiced after the supply. The most common examples
are utility invoices (e.g. light and heat, telephone) and any
other one-off payments such as lawyers and auditors fees.
Accruals are normally a relatively small balance on the financial
statements of a company which means audit work is limited.

 ## 2 - Relevance to 27/4Books

Accruals in 27/4Books relate mainly to utility invoices, audit fees, unpaid taxation
(wages, sales and company (corporation) taxes payable to the government).

Only minimal audit work will be required because the balance is quite small.

3 - Analytical review

This procedure will normally be limited to:

Example procedure	Relevance to 27/4Books
Review of individual balances	Comparing accruals balances this year to last year. Any changes should be in line with expectations e.g. if telephone charges have increased by say 5% then the accrual should also be 5% higher.

4 - Basic audit work on accruals

| Obtain list of accruals and cast | Compare to previous year to ensure balances are about the same | Agree larger balances to supporting documentation | Agree balances via nominal ledger to financial statements |

Stage	Point
②	Any significant change will be investigated by asking client staff/directors for an explanation.
③	Supporting documentation means the relevant invoice. For example, audit fees can be agreed to an invoice received after the end of the year. Similarly electricity invoices will be received after the year end. Some apportionment of electricity invoices may be needed – an invoice received at the end of January may relate to the period November to January, so for a December year-end an accrual of only 2/3 of the amount will be needed.

7.13 Bank and cash

1 - What are they?

Bank and cash relate to the monetary assets held by a company.

2 - Relevance to 27/4Books

The bank and cash balances will be those shown in the cash and bank books at 27/4Books. For the bank account, this may not be the amount actually at the bank due to "reconciling items"; see below for work on the bank reconciliation.

For our client, the main thing we need to make sure of is that the cash and bank balances belong to 27/4Books (the company has the rights to those amounts) and then that amounts are completely and accurately disclosed in the financial statements. The cash and bank balance is $489,000 – which is material so audit work is needed. Although there is no split of the balance between cash and bank, cash balances are normally very small – cash being held to pay for small items like drinks for the workplace and possibly small items of stationery. The emphasis is therefore on audit procedures for bank.

3 - Analytical procedures

Example procedure	Relevance to 27/4Books
Expectations	The directors stated that 27/4Books had a fairly good year which has been confirmed by higher sales and net profit being maintained. The amount of cash in the company, barring non-current asset purchases, should be about the same or perhaps more than last year.
Last year's figures	Bank balances have fallen by3% ($506k to $489k). This is surprising given the net profit for the year and lack of purchase of any non-current assets. However, payables have not increased as much as expected indicating that 27/4Books may be paying payables too quickly reducing the cash in the company.
Review of individual balances	As there will normally only be one bank account balance and perhaps a small petty cash balance, this procedure is not really relevant to cash and bank.
Real world	Overall sales in the book industry appear to be increasing as more people read books that have become films. We would therefore expect an increase in profit and cash in the company.

4 - Assertions relating to bank

The table below provides a summary of the audit approach to bank and cash. The key audit procedures of the "bank confirmation letter" and "bank reconciliation" are explained after the table.

Assertion	Audit objective	What could go wrong?	How do I ensure this error has not happened?	Audit procedure	Why does this procedure work?
Existence	The money is "real", that is it does exist.	The cash has been stolen so it is no longer there (unlikely but it is difficult to get an example here).	Obtain third party evidence on the existence of bank amounts. Where material, actually see the cash.	Bank confirmation letter. Count petty cash.	The bank confirmation provides third party evidence that the bank is real and also confirms any cash and other balances held by the bank.
Rights and obligations	The money belongs to the company.	The company is holding cash on behalf of another company.	Look for some evidence of ownership of the money.	Bank confirmation letter.	The letter will state the monetary amounts held at the bank for the company – effectively confirming ownership.
Completeness	All money balances are complete; there are none missing meaning money is understated.	A company has not included a bank account in the financial statements.	Obtain some evidence confirming that no amounts are missing.	Bank confirmation letter.	The bank letter lists all bank accounts held by the company effectively confirming completeness.
Valuation and allocation	The amount shown for monetary balances is correct – that is bank/cash are not over-stated.	Foreign currency bank balances are included at the wrong translation amount in the financial statements.	This error is extremely unlikely with standard cash and bank balances. It is a possibility with some financial instruments such as derivatives.	Bank confirmation letter. Count petty cash. Bank reconciliation.	The bank confirms the bank balances. Where the company has a lot of cash (e.g. a foreign exchange dealer) then count the money to ensure that the amount is correct.

Audit procedures for bank

The important audit procedures relating to bank are:

1. Bank confirmation letter, and

2. Bank reconciliation.

Although there are other procedures that can be used, these are the most important regarding examination preparation and provide the most coverage of audit assertions.

Bank confirmation letter

What is this?	Assertions covered	Explanation of assertion
The response to a letter sent from the auditor to the bank of the client to obtain details of the client's relationship with that bank. ISA505 provides guidance on the audit procedures relating to this letter.	Existence	The bank replies to the bank confirmation letter confirming that the bank balance actually exists.
	Rights and obligations	The bank confirms all the bank accounts, loans etc held at the bank in the client's name confirming ownership.
	Completeness	The bank provides details on all known bank accounts – if the client has missed an account that fact will be discovered by comparing accounts on the letter with those in the books of the client. Accounts at completely new banks will still be missed!
	Valuation and allocation	Valuation issues with bank accounts mainly relate to interest payable or receivable at the year end, not yet charged by the bank. Again the bank letter provides this information.

How to obtain a bank confirmation letter

Here are the five stages of obtaining a bank confirmation letter.

①	②	③	④	⑤
Auditor prepares standard bank letter	Client signs letter to authorise disclosure of information to the auditor	Auditor sends letter to the bank	Bank replies to the auditor	Auditor compares bank letter reply with client books

A couple of points about the bank letter:

Stage	Point
③ and ④	As with a receivables circularisation, the auditor sends the letter and receives the reply to ensure that the client does not amend any details on the letter.
⑤	Comparison includes ensuring that bank balances are correctly stated in terms of value and that all appropriate disclosures have been made in the financial statements. Important disclosures include any charges the bank has over company assets and loan repayment terms.

Main items referred to in a bank confirmation letter

A useful checklist – this can often be a small question in an auditing examination.

Items in bank letter	Reason for
Client name and address.	Confirms that the bank is replying concerning your client e.g. 27/4Books in this case!
List of bank accounts (current and deposit) held at bank with balance at the year end.	Confirms the completeness of balances in the financial statements and the accuracy of the balance
Details of loans from the bank including repayment dates and any charges over assets for security.	Confirms the completeness of loans in the financial statements and disclosure of loan terms where required (e.g. the repayment dates and charges)
Interest charged or payable not included in the account balances.	Interest charged will be an accrual and interest payment a prepayment; so these confirm partly the completeness of accruals and prepayments.
Assets held for safekeeping.	Examples here include title deeds for property and other valuable items such as gold watches (as in retirement gifts for employees – this does happen). Title deeds provide evidence of ownership of non-current assets while other assets will need to be disclosed as appropriate on the Statement of Financial Position.
Where known, details of bank accounts at other banks.	To confirm the completeness of bank information in the financial statements.

A note on bank reconciliations

A bank reconciliation is used to agree the balance in the company's cash book with balance shown on the bank statement. There used to be two main reasons for the cash book balance being different to the bank balance:

- firstly, regarding cheque payments. There was a delay while the cheque worked its way through the postal service to the payee, then further delay as the cheque was banked and finally worked its way through the banking system back to the cheque writers bank account

- secondly, cheques received. Cheques would be received by a company in payment of goods sold. The cheque was paid in at the bank, but would not be "cleared" that is the money could not be spent, until the cheque had worked its way through the banking system back to the account of the person writing that cheque.

These delays meant that the company's bank account balance was different from the that shown at the bank because:

- cheques written would be immediately deducted from the company's bank account but only from the bank in about a week

- cheques received would be immediately added to the company's bank account, but only at the bank after they had "cleared" – taking about 4 days

Of course, most receipts and payments now are by bank transfer. Monies paid leave the bank on the same day they are entered into the cash book. Monies received are "cleared funds" – there is no delay in waiting for a cheque to go through the banking system. This means that bank reconciliations become less important from the audit point-of-view – and why I've only provided this summary to explain them now.

A note on counting petty cash

Most companies maintain what is called a "petty cash" balance; that is a small amount of cash to purchase sundry small items like drinks for office staff or items of stationery such as pens and pencils. The auditor may decide to count this balance at the year-end, but as petty cash is normally very small (and therefore immaterial) then this is unlikely.

7.14 Non-current assets

1 - What are they?

Non-current assets are assets purchased by a company which are used over a number of years to assist the company in manufacturing the products it makes or delivering the services it provides.

2 - Relevance to 27/4Books

In 27/4Books, the main non-current assets are the warehouse where books are stored prior to re-sale and fork-lift trucks used for moving books around in the warehouse.

For our client, the main thing we need to make sure of is that the non-current assets belong to 27/4Books (the company has the rights to those assets) and then that amounts are completely and accurately disclosed in the financial statements. The non-current assets balance is $653,000 – which is material so audit work is needed.

3 - Analytical procedures

Example procedure	Relevance to 27/4Books
Expectations	The directors stated that 27/4Books had a fairly good year although budgets show that no new non-current assets were due to be purchased. Overall, the net book value of non-current assets will be less than last year due to depreciation of plant and machinery.
Last year's figures	Non-current assets have fallen by roughly 7% ($698k to $653k) which was expected as no new assets have been purchased.
Review of individual balances	Individual balances are not given for this example, but the auditor would normally investigate: • new non-current assets (none this year) • a random sample of the remaining balances.
Real world	Overall sales in the book industry appear to be increasing as more people read books that have become films.

4 - Assertions relating to non-current assets

The table below provides a summary of the audit approach to non-current assets. The key audit procedures are standard to most audits; those procedures are summarised after this table.

Assertion	Audit objective	What could go wrong?	How do I ensure this error has not happened?	Audit procedure	Why does this procedure work?
Existence	The non-current assets are "real", that they do exist.	Assets sold during the year and not removed from the accounts.	Select some non-current assets from the asset register and see them.	See the assets at the inventory count or as a separate procedure on the final audit.	Actually seeing the assets confirms that they do exist.
Rights and obligations	The non-current assets belong to the company.	The non-current assets do not belong to the company e.g. held on an operating lease.	Obtain some evidence of ownership or title to the assets.	See relevant ownership documents.	A document such as a title deed for a building shows who is the actual owner of the asset.
Completeness	All non-current assets are complete; that is none are missing so there is no under-statement.	Non-current assets are included in repairs and renewals.	See the non-current assets and confirm recording in non-current asset records of the company.	Obtain asset details on the inventory count.	These details can be agreed back to the non-current assets register after the inventory count. Any assets not found in the ledger indicate that the register is incomplete and the asset was therefore not recorded.
Valuation and allocation	The amount shown for non-current assets is correct – that is non-current assets values are not over or under-stated.	Non-current assets have been incorrectly depreciated / amortised resulting in an incorrect valuation.	Audit the depreciation policy of the company to ensure rates charged are appropriate.	Analytical procedures / re-calculation of depreciation charges AND profit / losses on sale.	Comparison of the depreciation charges to prior year, other companies and industry standards confirms the overall accuracy of the charge. Large profits/losses on sale are indicative of incorrect depreciation – see below.

Audit procedures on non-current assets

There are various audit procedures on non-current assets that will always be carried out. These procedures are summarised below:

Audit procedure	Brief explanation	Assertion tested	Why?
Seeing assets at the inventory count (1).	Before the inventory count, obtain details of some assets from the non-current assets register. At the count, inspect the assets.	Existence	Seeing the asset proves it exists.
Seeing assets at the inventory count (2).	At the inventory count, record details of some of the non-current assets. After the count, ensure that the assets are recorded in the non-current assets register.	Completeness	Tracing the non-current asset into the register confirms the asset has been recorded (and the non-current asset register is complete).
Obtaining title deeds for land and buildings.	For land and buildings recorded in the non-current asset register, see the title deeds (or confirm that the bank confirmation letter lists those deeds).	Rights and obligations	The deed provides evidence of ownership and therefore the right of 27/4Books to use that asset.
Re-calculation of depreciation calculation.	For a sample of assets in the non-current asset register, re-calculate the depreciation charge.	Valuation	Ensures the accuracy of the depreciation charge.
Re-calculation of profit/losses on sale of non-current assets.	For a sample of non-current assets sold during the year, re-calculate the profit/loss.	Valuation	Large profits or losses suggest over- or under depreciation of non-current assets. Checking profits/losses therefore provides a guide to the accuracy of the deprecation charge.
Analytical review of depreciation.	Compare the depreciation charge for each type of non-current asset this year to prior years. Ask the directors to explain any unusual changes in the amount of depreciation charged or changes to the depreciation policy.	Valuation and allocation	Helps to confirm the overall accuracy of the depreciation charge.

Audit procedure	Brief explanation	Assertion tested	Why?
Tests to ensure that the non-current assets register is correct.	Various tests including: • agreeing purchase of non-current assets from PDB to the register • agreeing sale of non-current assets from register to SDB • adding up the register and agreeing balances to the financial statements (specifically the non-current assets note).	Completeness and allocation	Confirms the accuracy of the register in terms of assets in the register as well as the mathematical accuracy of the register.

7.15 A note on share capital

1 - What is this?

Share capital represents the amount invested in a company by it's shareholders. Technically, share capital is the nominal amount or face value of the shares. Any additional purchase amount is credited to a share premium account (and I'll leave explanation of share premium accounts to your financial accounting studies).

2 - Relevance to 27/4Books

In 27/4Books, as in most companies, share capital does not change from year-to-year. In this case, audit work will be limited to simply ensuring that the same information as last year on shares is disclosed in the financial statements.

Where share capital does change, that is new shares are issued, the auditor will normally verify the receipt of cash to the cash book and ensure that the share capital balance on the financial statements is increased to show the new value.

7.16 A note on reserves

1 - What are these?

 Reserves are the profits/losses a company has accumulated over its years of trading.

2 -  Relevance to 27/4Books

In 27/4Books, as in many companies, reserves are a significant figure on the Statement of Financial Position showing that 27/4Books has been profitable in the past. However, this does not mean audit work is extensive. The auditor will normally confirm that the opening balance on reserves agrees to last year's financial statements, and that the movement on reserves agrees to the Income Statement. Apart from more advanced accounting reasons (which as with share capital I will leave to your financial accounting studies) that is the only change that will take place on reserves during the year.

7.17 So where are we now?

At the end of the most detailed chapter in this book (since the last one!).

You have learnt about Statement of Financial Position auditing (or at least now have an idea about what happens).

As with chapter 6, treat this chapter as a reference work – when you are learning about auditing of assets and liabilities, go back to this chapter and refresh your memory on the audit of that asset/liability.

7.18 Summary of the summary

Finally the chapter summary; succinct and to the point:

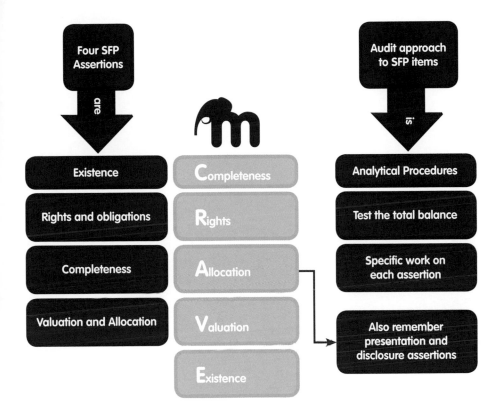

Chapter 8

The audit cycle
closedown

A student's guide to Auditing By Alan Lewin

8.1 Introduction – what will you learn?

We are now getting towards the end of the audit. You can almost imagine the auditor racing on from the end of Income Statement (IS) and Statement of Financial Position (SFP) audit testing, towards the "goal" of being able to write the audit report, but being diverted into doing other small but nevertheless important jobs.

In other words, these audit procedures take place at the end of the audit when IS and SFP testing is complete. There are 6 more things that the auditor must do and using our car analogy, these are:

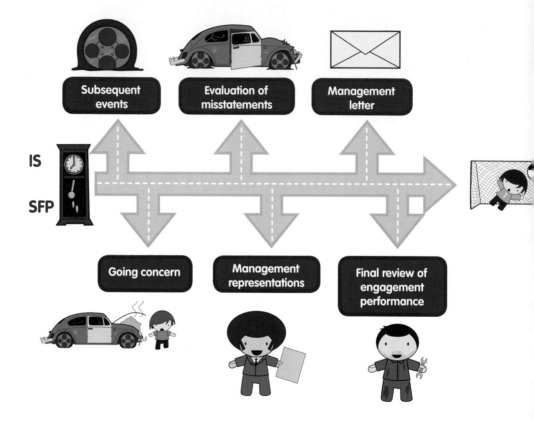

In overview, these diversions are:

Event		Car example	Audit relevance	Section reference
	Subsequent events	Making sure nothing has happened after the end of the year to affect the running of the car (like punctures that could have been foreseen due to illegal tyres).	Events after the year end affecting the financial statements that mean that financial statements need amendment.	8.3
	Going concern	Ensure the car will continue to work into the future.	The company should be able to continue for the "foreseeable future".	8.4
	Evaluation of misstatements	Keeping a record of faults discovered in our car.	Making sure any errors found in the financial statements are not material.	8.5
	Management representations	Checking that the person selling the car told the truth (i.e. that the car is fit for purpose – and roadworthy).	Asking the directors to confirm that the financial statements are correct.	8.6
	Management letter	Writing back to the car seller with information about problems found.	Writing to the management to inform them of control weaknesses.	8.7
	Final review of performance	Checking "under the bonnet" to ensure that the mechanic has maintained the car correctly.	Review of audit work and procedures to ensure audit firm standards were followed.	8.8

Note though that these jobs do not necessarily take place one at a time; they will probably run concurrently. It is just simpler to explain them individually.

8.2 So, what is in this chapter?

Specifically this chapter covers the six important areas of an audit from completion of audit testing to just before the auditor signs the audit report.

Each of these sections has an ISA to outline the audit work. As in other chapters, that ISA is summarised and where possible explained in plain English terms.

8.3 Subsequent events

This is where we ensure our car has not been affected by accidents we could have foreseen (like illegal tyres) or in audit terms looking for events after the financial statements date that need to be shown in those financial statements.

Overview of the ISA

 Subsequent events are explained in ISA 560 *Subsequent Events*. The ISA explains the work of an auditor for events occurring after the date of the financial statements.

Key things you must understand are:

1. the two different types of subsequent events, examples of them and the normal accounting treatment

2. the auditor's objectives regarding subsequent events, and

3. how the work of an auditor differs depending on when the event took place.

These things are explained in the next sections.

Types of subsequent events

ISA 560 recognises two types of subsequent events (useful as IAS 10 does exactly the same!).

d ISA Definition	Plain English explanation	Example	Normal accounting treatment
Event 1 Those events that provide evidence of conditions that existed at the date of the financial statements .	Literally look at the financial statements and think whether the event could be seen from the detail in the financials; if so the financial statements need to be amended for that event. These events used to be called "adjusting events" because the financial statements need amendment for the event.	Provision against year-end inventory or receivables. In 27/4Books this would be a receivable going "bad" that is unable to pay amounts due to 27/4Books. The year-end value of that receivable is probably zero rather than the amount originally stated.	Adjust the financial statements, normally with a provision.
Event 2 Those events that provide evidence of conditions that arose after the date of the financial statements.	These are events which could not be foreseen at the date of the financial statements – and so any liability does not belong to that accounting period. These events also used to be called "non-adjusting events" because there is no financial effect on the financial statements.	Liabilities being incurred after the end of the year. In 27/4Books this could be a delivery lorry accidently hitting the warehouse – which would then need repairing. The repair cost relates to the year that the accident occurred.	Do not adjust the financial statements although a disclosure note of the event may be required so the users are aware of the situation.

Auditor's objectives

The auditor has two objectives regarding subsequent events:

- firstly, to obtain sufficient evidence about events occurring between the date of the financial statements and the date of the audit report to decide whether adjustment and/or disclosure of the event is required

- secondly, after the date of the audit report, to decide whether information provided to the auditor at this time means that the auditors' report may need changing.

These objectives are reflected in the audit work explained below.

Events at different dates

According to the ISA, subsequent events can actually occur in three different time periods after the end of the year. Audit work is different depending on the timing of the subsequent event.

The timings of events are shown below

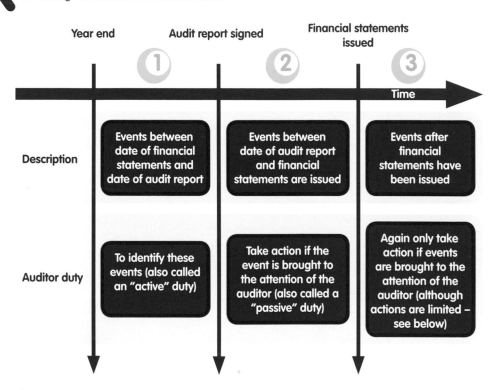

	Year end	Audit report signed	Financial statements issued
	①	②	③
Description	Events between date of financial statements and date of audit report	Events between date of audit report and financial statements are issued	Events after financial statements have been issued
Auditor duty	To identify these events (also called an "active" duty)	Take action if the event is brought to the attention of the auditor (also called a "passive" duty)	Again only take action if events are brought to the attention of the auditor (although actions are limited – see below)

Audit work and action that the auditor can take are described below for each event.

Events between the year end and the signing of the audit report (①)

Audit work and actions the auditor can take at this time are:

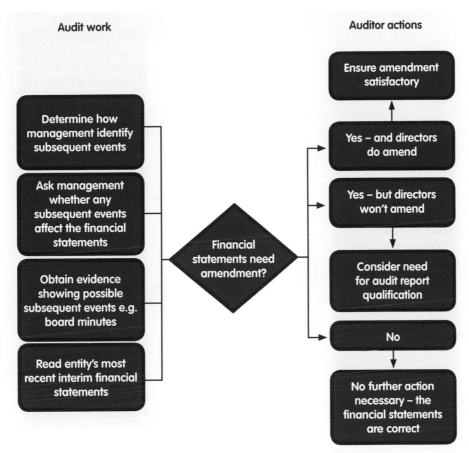

Audit work

- Determine how management identify subsequent events
- Ask management whether any subsequent events affect the financial statements
- Obtain evidence showing possible subsequent events e.g. board minutes
- Read entity's most recent interim financial statements

Financial statements need amendment?

Auditor actions

- Ensure amendment satisfactory
- Yes – and directors do amend
- Yes – but directors won't amend
- Consider need for audit report qualification
- No
- No further action necessary – the financial statements are correct

The auditor will also obtain a management representation letter point confirming that all subsequent events are adjusted/disclosed as necessary in the financial statements. See section 8.6 for detail on management representations.

Events between signing of the audit report and issuing of financial statements (2)

Audit work and actions the auditor can take at this time are:

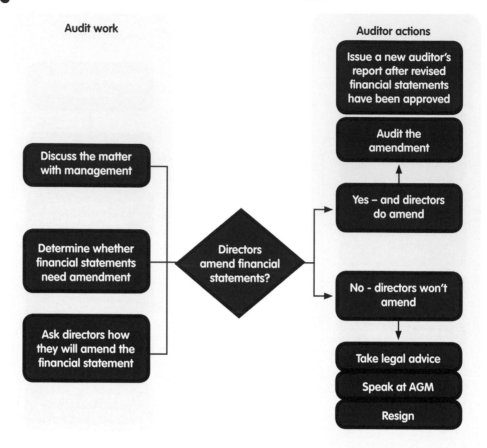

As the audit report has already been issued, following an adjustment/disclosure of a subsequent event a new report is required. However, if the directors won't amend the financial statements the auditor has a problem; the financial statements lack vital information for the shareholders but the directors won't disclose this. The only options for the auditor include taking legal advice, speaking at the AGM or as a last resort resigning. Remember resignation will normally allow the auditor to require the directors to convene a General Meeting – so the auditor can tell the members about the problems with the financial statements.

Events after the issuing of the financial statements ( )

Audit work and actions the auditor can take at this time are:

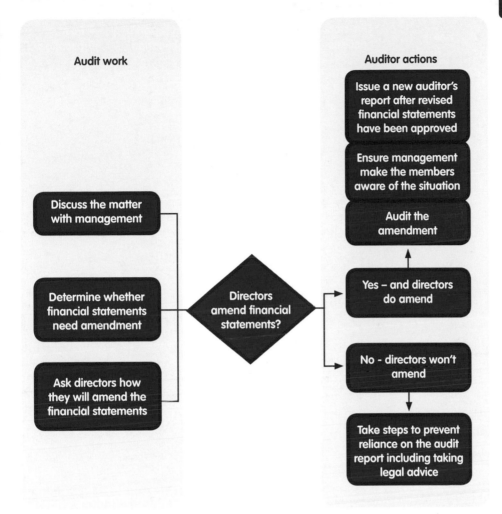

Audit work at this time is the same as situation ② above. However, actions are different:

- if the directors amend the financial statements, not only does the auditor have to audit the amendment and re-issue the audit report, but also ensure members are made aware of the need for amended financial statements

- if management won't amend the financial statements then speaking at the AGM is normally no longer an option – this has already happened. The auditor therefore takes legal advice and takes action to try and avoid reliance being placed on the report. The ISA does not state what this action can be.

Summary of subsequent events

To summarise, normal audit work on subsequent events is as follows:

Event	Directors actions	Financial statements date to audit report	Audit report to publication	Post – publication
Evidence of conditions at financial statements date.	Directors amend/disclose	Audit amendment	Audit amendment and re-issue audit report	Ensure members know of change, audit amendment and re-issue audit report
	Directors do not amend/ disclose	Qualify audit report if material	Take legal advice, speak at AGM	Take legal advice and attempt to publicise incorrect financial statements
No evidence of conditions at financial statements date.	Directors disclose event if necessary	Ensure disclosure is sufficient	Audit disclosure and re-issue audit report	Ensure members know of change, audit disclosure and re-issue audit report
	Directors do nothing but disclosure necessary	Qualify audit report if material	Take legal advice, speak at AGM	Take legal advice and attempt to publicise incorrect financial statements

Finally, remember that the auditor will always obtain a letter of representation point confirming that the financial statements have appropriate disclosure/amendment for all known subsequent events.

8.4 Going concern

This is where we ensure our car can continue working for another year, or in audit terms, that our client company will be existence for the "foreseeable future".

Overview of the ISA

 Audit work on the going concern assumption is explained in ISA 570 *Going Concern*. The ISA explains the work of an auditor in ensuring that the company being audited will (hopefully) continue to be a going concern.

Key things you must understand are:

1. the auditor's objectives regarding going concern

2. audit procedures relating to the going concern assumption, and

3. reporting problems with going concern.

These things are explained in the next sections.

Auditor's objectives

The main objective of the auditor regarding going concern is to literally ensure that the entity being audited is a going concern. Hopefully you recall from your financial accounting studies that an entity is viewed as continuing in business for the foreseeable future unless there are reasons to suggest this will not be the case.

Reasons the going concern assumption will not be used are simply:

1. the entity is in liquidation or has ceased operations, or

2. management have no alternative but to cease operations.

The specific objectives that the auditor must follow are:

d ISA Statement	Plain English statement
To obtain sufficient appropriate audit evidence regarding the appropriateness of management's use of the going concern assumption in the preparation of the financial statements.	The auditor will collect audit evidence to confirm that the financial statements should be prepared using the going concern assumption.
To conclude, based on the audit evidence obtained, whether a material uncertainty exists related to events or conditions that may cast significant doubt on the entity's ability to continue as a going concern; and	Using the audit evidence obtained, decide whether or not the company is a going concern.
To determine the implications for the auditor's report.	If the company is unlikely to be a going concern, or information about the going concern status is not fully disclosed in the financial statements, then the auditor may need to amend the audit report to provide this information.

Audit work on the going concern assumption (part 1)

As mentioned, the main aim of the auditor is to ensure that the entity being audited is a going concern. Initially audit work takes on two themes:

1. Identifying going concern indicators	2. Discussing with management their going concern assessment
As the audit progresses, the auditor will make a note of any factors which *suggest* the company may be having going concern problems. For example: • the company is loss making • key staff are leaving • greater reliance placed on bank loans • there are net current liabilities • loss of major customers.	The company's management should be assessing the company's ability to continue as a going concern and producing evidence to support this. However, that assessment is affected by: • how far significant events are in the future (further into the future means more uncertainty) • how large and complex the entity is (larger and more complex means more uncertainty) • other uncertain future events (such as interest rate changes).

If there are indicators that the entity may not be a going concern then additional audit procedures are carried out – as explained in the next section.

Audit work on the going concern assumption (part 2)

The auditor is now attempting to show that the entity is a going concern by obtaining other additional relevant evidence.

Audit procedure	Why carried out
1. If not already carried out, ask management to make an assessment of the entity's ability to continue as a going concern.	To ensure management are aware of the need to review the going concern status of the company.
2. Evaluate management action plans to ensure the entity can continue trading.	To ensure that management have made a realistic assessment of the company's ability to remain a going concern.
3. Evaluate any cash flow forecasts ensuring that the basis of the forecast is reasonable.	To ensure the company has sufficient cash to survive. Cash flow is important to any business. Primary evidence of going concern problems is a lack of cash, now or in the future.
4. Reviewing any other data obtained since managements' going concern assessment.	To ensure that the auditor has sufficient evidence to form an opinion on the going concern assumption. This evidence may include other going concern indicators, as already mentioned above.
5. Obtaining a management representation point on the ability of the entity to continue as a going concern.	Although not persuasive evidence regarding the entity's ability to survive, the representation point does remind management that they are responsible for the going concern position of the entity.

After collecting all the evidence, the auditor must decide whether or not the going concern assumption is valid for the company being audited.

e Going concern of 27/4Books

For our audit client, there are few, if any, going concern issues. The company is making a profit and there is little reliance on bank loans so audit work is likely to be limited to:

*   ensuring that the directors do carry out a going concern assessment

*   reviewing this assessment to ensure it is appropriate

*   obtaining a representation letter point.

d Reporting on going concern

The auditor needs to ask three questions to determine the type of audit report on the going concern assumptions. These questions are shown below along with the appropriate audit report. You will find more detail on audit reports in chapter 9 – so you may want to book-mark this page and return to it after reading that chapter.

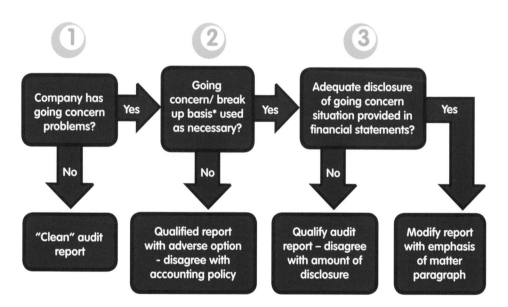

*Break up basis means that the financial statements are prepared as if the company is not a going concern - that is assets are being sold and the company will cease to exist.

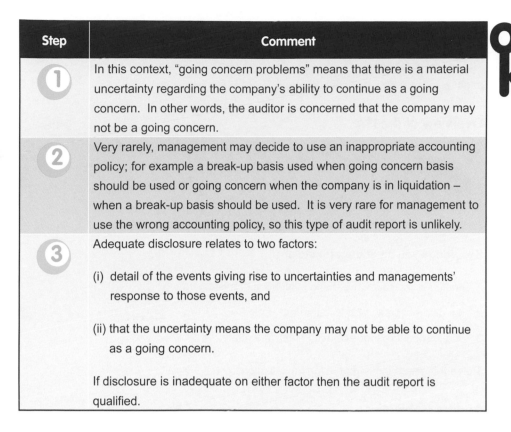

Step	Comment
1	In this context, "going concern problems" means that there is a material uncertainty regarding the company's ability to continue as a going concern. In other words, the auditor is concerned that the company may not be a going concern.
2	Very rarely, management may decide to use an inappropriate accounting policy; for example a break-up basis used when going concern basis should be used or going concern when the company is in liquidation – when a break-up basis should be used. It is very rare for management to use the wrong accounting policy, so this type of audit report is unlikely.
3	Adequate disclosure relates to two factors: (i) detail of the events giving rise to uncertainties and managements' response to those events, and (ii) that the uncertainty means the company may not be able to continue as a going concern. If disclosure is inadequate on either factor then the audit report is qualified.

Summary of going concern

The auditor will:

1. assess the company to determine whether there are any going concern indicators (that is anything suggesting that the company is not a going concern)

2. where going concern indicators exist, perform additional audit procedures to try to determine the company's going concern status, and

3. modify the audit report where there is doubt about the going concern assumption.

8.5 Evaluation of misstatements

This is where we keep a record of any faults found with our car after purchase, or in audit terms make a record of any errors found in the financial statements.

Overview of the ISA

The evaluation of misstatements is explained in ISA 450 *Evaluation of Misstatements Identified During the Audit.* The ISA explains how an auditor responds to misstatements found during the audit.

Key things you must understand are:

1. auditor's objectives regarding evaluation of misstatements

2. the different types of misstatements, and

3. audit procedures for evaluating misstatements.

These things are explained in the next sections.

Auditor's objectives

Remember as the auditor carries out audit work, a schedule of misstatements will be produced. Towards the end of the audit this schedule is reviewed, discussed with management and where necessary amendments recommended in the financial statements.

There are two main objectives for the auditor regarding misstatements mentioned in the ISA.

d ISA Statement	Plain English statement
The auditor will evaluate the effect of identified misstatements on the audit.	During the audit the auditor maintains a list of misstatements found during audit work. Towards the end of the audit, this list will be reviewed and management will normally be asked to amend the financial statements – especially where the misstatements in total are material.
The auditor will evaluate the effect of uncorrected misstatements, if any, on the financial statements.	After all amendments have been made to the financial statements by management, the auditor will find the total effect of any remaining misstatements and if material consider qualifying the audit report.

It is important to be clear on the term "misstatement". The term appears to refer only to money – but that is not the case here. For this ISA, a misstatement refers to:

- amounts
- classification
- disclosure, or
- presentation

of items in the financial statements. A misstatement therefore occurs when an item is not shown correctly regarding amount, classification, disclosure or presentation according to the financial reporting framework in force.

Misstatements could relate to any of the examples below:

Misstatement	Example of misstatement	Correct treatment in financial statements
Amount	Inventory amount includes old inventory valued at $500,000.	Inventory amount should be shown net of a provision.
Classification	Inventory is included in the financial statements as "receivables".	Inventory should be included under the financial statements heading "inventory".
Disclosure / Presentation	Inventory is stated as being valued at selling price (when it is not).	Inventory should be stated as valued at the lower of cost and net realisable value.

Note in ISA 315, disclosure and presentation assertions are shown together with no separate definition so they are not split here.

Finally, uncorrected misstatements are any misstatements that the auditor has found during the audit which have not been corrected by management. If these misstatement are material then the auditor may well have to qualify the audit report.

Procedure for evaluating misstatements

The audit procedure for evaluating misstatements is shown below:

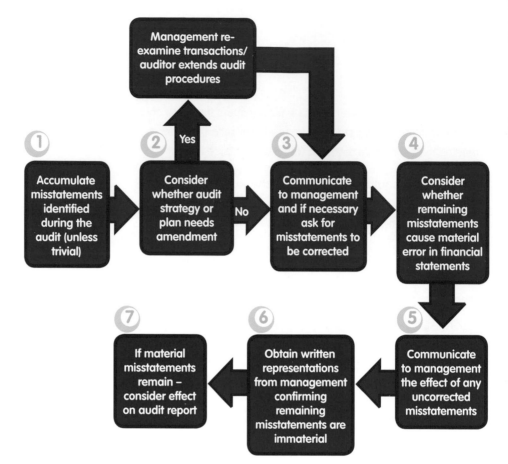

Step	Comment
1	As you may expect, small or trivial misstatements are ignored.
2	For larger misstatements, the audit strategy or audit plan may need to be amended and additional audit evidence obtained. This may be to try to obtain a more precise value on the amount of any misstatement – which in turn helps with identifying material errors.
3	Management will normally amend the financial statements (remember the auditor cannot do this – the financial statements are the responsibility of management). However, if management choose not to amend the financial statements, the auditor will need to document reasons for this.
4	The auditor needs to know whether remaining misstatements cause material error so management can be warned of the possibility of audit qualification.
5	Management are told of the remaining errors.
6	Management then confirm the amount of those errors back to the auditor (see the next section in this chapter on written representations).
7	Finally, remaining material errors may result in qualification (see chapter 9 for more details on qualifications).

Summary of evaluation of misstatements

The auditor will:

1. collect details of misstatements found during the audit

2. at the end of the audit, discuss those misstatements with management

3. management normally correct the financial statements for misstatements, and

4. any remaining material misstatements will normally cause the auditor to qualify the audit report.

8.6 Management representations

This is where we ask the person selling the car to confirm that the car is roadworthy, or in audit terms the auditor asks the directors to confirm that the financial statements are actually correct.

Overview of the ISA

Management letters are explained in ISA 580 *Written Representations*. The ISA explains how an auditor obtains evidence from the company's management about specific aspects of those financial statements.

This letter is commonly called a management representation letter – because this is where the management make various representations to the auditor about the audit of the financial statements.

Key things you must understand are:

Auditor's objectives:

1. why the letter is written

2. the procedure for writing the letter

3. what the basic contents of the letter are, and

4. how to overcome problems in obtaining management representations.

These things are explained in the following sections.

Auditor's objectives

The main reason that auditors require a management letter is the difficulty of ensuring that audit evidence collected during an audit is complete and accurate. As management control a company, it would be relatively easy for them to hide evidence or provide the auditor with misleading information (just think how the management of Enron managed to "hide" liabilities in off-shore companies).

The slightly sarcastic view here is "if management are going to lie, then get them to lie in writing" – in other words if the financial statements are later found to be incorrect, at least the auditor has evidence that the management said the statements were true. This will provide some minimal defence in court against auditor negligence.

Bearing this in mind, here are the requirements from the ISA with the plain English statement referring back to the view that auditors need appropriate evidence to protect themselves from managements' (possible) lies.

d ISA Statement	Plain English statement
To obtain written representations from management and, where appropriate, those charged with governance that they believe that they have fulfilled their responsibility for the preparation of the financial statements and for the completeness of the information provided to the auditor.	The auditor will obtain a letter from company management basically confirming that: • nothing has been omitted from the financial statements and • the auditor has been given all the information needed to complete the audit.
To support other audit evidence relevant to the financial statements or specific assertions in the financial statements by means of written representations if determined necessary by the auditor or required by other ISAs.	The letter also contains any other statements required by the auditor (see below for a list of normal contents of a representation letter).
To respond appropriately to written representations provided by management and, where appropriate, those charged with governance, or if management or, where appropriate, those charged with governance do not provide the written representations requested by the auditor.	If necessary, the auditor will: • respond to the representation letter (for example due to lack of completeness of points made or unclear wording), and • consider what action to take if a representation letter is not provided by management.

Obtaining a representation letter

A management representation letter is obtained as follows:

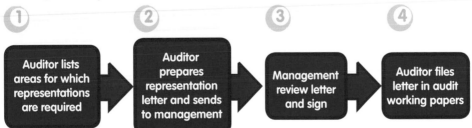

Note that the letter is obtained as close as possible to the date the audit report is signed. This means that audit evidence is as up-to-date as possible when the report is signed. Any delay in signing the report may mean another representation letter is required.

Contents of a representation letter

Representation letters include two "sets" or lists of representations:

1. Those specifically required by the ISA, and

2. Other representations that the auditor considers necessary.

although the representation letter itself may not make any distinction between the lists.

Representation	Why it is there
Specifically from the ISA	
Management confirms it has fulfilled its responsibility for the preparation of the financial statements in accordance with the applicable financial reporting framework, including, where relevant, the fair presentation of those financial statements, as set out in the terms of the audit engagement.	The completeness and accuracy of the financial statements is the responsibility of management. Although the auditor does report on compliance with the financial reporting framework and the fairness of the financial statements (see chapter 9 on audit reporting), getting the management to confirm this in writing gives the auditor appropriate evidence that this actually is the case.
Management has provided the auditor with all relevant information and access as agreed in the terms of the audit engagement.	It is difficult for the auditor to know if management have actually given the auditor all the information requested or required by the auditor. If it comes to light later that management have hidden information or lied to the auditor, there is written evidence that they did not do this!
All transactions have been recorded and are reflected in the Financial Statements.	It is impossible for the auditor to verify that the financial statements are complete (as already noted management can "hide" transactions); although completeness is an assertion that the auditor has to comply with. The auditor therefore asks the directors to confirm this assertion – after all, the financial statements are the responsibility of the directors!
Other representations	
The auditor may consider it necessary to request other written representations about the financial statements. These include: • plans of the company • details of liabilities (actual and contingent) • going concern status of the entity • representations on specific audit assertions (e.g. valuation of investments).	Again, only the management run the company and the auditor is only gaining appropriate written evidence about various management decisions concerning the company.

This list can be a useful in an auditing examination where a question asks for indicative contents of a management letter.

 27/4Books management letter

27/4Books is a relatively standard audit. However, representations that will normally be required from management in addition to those that must be obtained from the ISA, will include:

- the amount of any provision against inventories
- the amount of any provision against receivables, and
- confirmation that the directors have applied accounting standards and chosen appropriate accounting policies including depreciation rates.

As these matters include some element of judgement, the auditor requires management to confirm these decisions in writing.

Issues in obtaining management representations

There are various problems in obtaining management representations. The major problems and potential actions by the auditor are shown below:

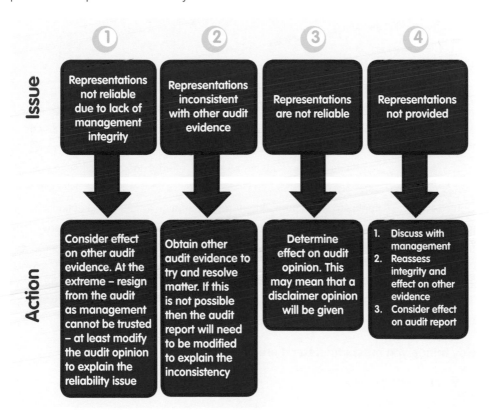

	①	②	③	④
Issue	Representations not reliable due to lack of management integrity	Representations inconsistent with other audit evidence	Representations are not reliable	Representations not provided
Action	Consider effect on other audit evidence. At the extreme – resign from the audit as management cannot be trusted – at least modify the audit opinion to explain the reliability issue	Obtain other audit evidence to try and resolve matter. If this is not possible then the audit report will need to be modified to explain the inconsistency	Determine effect on audit opinion. This may mean that a disclaimer opinion will be given	1. Discuss with management 2. Reassess integrity and effect on other evidence 3. Consider effect on audit report

The main point to remember is that lack of representations or representations that appear to be unreliable mean the auditor will not have sufficient, appropriate audit evidence. This will almost certainly mean that the auditor is uncertain about some evidence obtained and the audit opinion will be qualified. Chapter 9 explains audit report qualifications.

Summary of representation letters

The auditor will:

1. decide on the areas where management representations are required

2. draft the letter for management

3. ensure management sign the letter as close as possible to the date of the audit report, and

4. if management won't sign the letter, or the auditor doubts the validity of the representations, then the audit report will normally be modified.

8.7 Management letters

This is where we write to the seller of the car to provide information on how well the car has performed, or in audit terms to inform management of weaknesses in their company's control systems.

Overview of the ISA

Management letters are explained in ISA 265 *Communicating Deficiencies in Internal Control to Those Charged With Governance and Management* (which is a long name for a small ISA so I'll keep on using the term "Management letter" to save on space). The ISA explains how an auditor can report internal control weaknesses to management.

Don't get this ISA confused with management representation letters (see section 8.6 in this chapter). The management representation letter is sent from the company management to the auditor; this letter is from the auditor to the company management.

The letter is also sometimes called the "letter of weakness" or "report to management". The clear distinction between the two letters is the word "*representation*"; this always refers to the letter from management to the auditor, which is not this letter!

Key things you must understand are:

1. why the letter is written

2. the procedure for writing the letter, and

3. what the basic contents of the letter are.

These things are explained in the next sections.

Auditor's objectives

There is one main objective for the auditor regarding management letters mentioned in the ISA.

d ISA Statement	Plain English statement
The objective of the auditor is to communicate appropriately to those charged with governance and management, deficiencies in internal control that the auditor has identified during the audit and that, in the auditor's professional judgment, are of sufficient importance to merit their respective attentions.	During an audit the auditor may find weaknesses in the internal control systems at the client. If any weakness is important – that is the control system may not work correctly – then the auditor will inform the client.

In other words, the management letter is written to help the client company improve its internal control systems. However, reporting is not optional; the ISA is explicit in stating the auditor shall report on internal control weaknesses.

The auditor is required to report on two things:

d ISA Statement: reporting requirement	Plain English statement
The auditor will report situations where: (i) a control is designed, implemented or operated in such a way that it is unable to prevent, or detect and correct, misstatements in the financial statements on a timely basis	The auditor will report on: (i) controls which cannot: • prevent – stop an error happening • detect – identify an error has occurred or • correct – take action to adjust for the control deficiency.
(ii) a control necessary to prevent, or detect and correct, misstatements in the financial statements on a timely basis is missing.	(ii) controls which should be in a company's control system to prevent errors occurring but are missing from that system.

In other words the auditor is assessing the control system in place, both for weaknesses in the controls actually there and for controls that should be there but are missing.

Procedure for writing a management letter

The ISA mentions two key questions in helping an auditor decide whether to report on internal control weaknesses, as shown below:

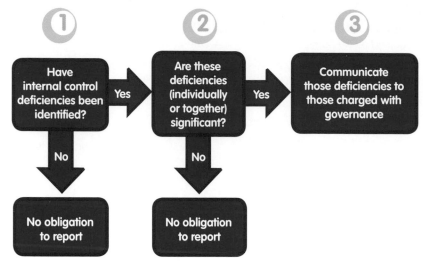

The meaning of the word "significant" in the second question is not defined – although the auditor could take this to mean "material". But, in many situations control deficiencies may not be proved to be material, so "significant" can simply mean "capable of producing a material error".

To be helpful to the client and provide added value to the audit, the auditor will normally report on most weaknesses found, unless they are minor or result from errors that are unlikely to be repeated.

The letter is written and sent at the end of the audit when audit work is complete. However, information for the letter will be collected throughout the audit by the audit team; it is then convenient to send one letter on audit completion, rather than many small letters during the audit.

Example content of a management letter

The ISA recommends that the auditor communicates:

1. a description of the weakness

2. an explanation of the potential effects of the weakness, and

3. optionally, suggestions on remedial action to overcome the weakness.

The best way to show the contents of a management letter is in an example. Back in chapter 6 we looked at the different transaction systems in 27/4Books. For each system, there was a table showing what could go wrong with the system and then the controls to try to ensure that each error had not occurred. If the error had occurred, then there would be an internal control weakness.

For example, in the sales system there was a computer control to ensure that despatch note information was transferred to the invoicing systems (see chapter 6). What if the computer didn't transfer information correctly – the control weakness would mean that either a customer was not invoiced or that a different customer (who didn't order the goods) was invoiced. Both of these errors are internal control weaknesses.

These weaknesses would be reported in the management letter as follows:

Weakness	Potential effect of weakness	Suggested remedial action
The computer control ensuring that goods despatch information was correctly transferred to the sales invoicing routine was found to be ineffective:		
• On 3 items tested, despatch information was not transferred.	Goods are despatched from 27/4Books but no sales invoice is produced. The sales figure is therefore understated in the Income Statement.	Improve computer controls. A sub-routine can be written to compare despatch note and sales invoice sequences (both sequences use the same reference number) and report breaks in the sequence for further investigation.
• On 2 items tested, the customer reference number was incorrectly transferred.	The sales invoice would be sent to the wrong customer resulting in non-payment of the invoice.	Improve computer controls. The customer reference number fields on the despatch note and the sales invoice should always be compared to ensure they are the same.

The tabular format is fine – both for "real" letters and in an examination situation. The presentation of the information is clear and from the exam point-of-view, it forces you to complete all three boxes for each weakness – checking completeness of the answer.

Summary of management letters

The auditor will:

1. identify control weaknesses during the audit

2. summarise those weaknesses at the end of the audit, and

3. write to the client company in a formal letter which

    a. identifies each weakness

    b. explains the potential effect of that weakness

    c. suggests action to overcome the weakness.

8.8 Final review of engagement performance

This is where we check "under the bonnet" to ensure that the mechanic has maintained the car correctly, or in audit terms that the audit has been performed in accordance with the correct standards.

Overview of the section / ISA

The final review of engagement performance is really to do with two things; quality control of the audit engagement and ensuring that the auditor has sufficient evidence to form the opinion on the financial statements.

The evaluation of engagement performance is explained in ISA 220 *Quality Control*. Part of this ISA explains actions to be taken at the end of the audit to ensure quality control has been maintained. The key sections of this ISA are summarised below.

Obtaining sufficient audit evidence has already been considered in chapter 5 regarding ISA 500. The need for sufficient evidence is mentioned here again, mainly as a checklist, just to confirm that the auditor does have sufficient evidence.

Key things you must understand are:

1. the three main areas of reviewing the engagement, and

2. audit evidence review.

Both of these points are explained overleaf.

Review of engagement

The review of the audit engagement has three sections:

1. engagement performance - engagement partner's review

2. quality control review, and

3. documentation review

These are explained below:

Engagement performance – engagement partner's review

The main focus on quality control at the end of the audit is the engagement partner's review of the audit work. Note this is a review of the audit work, not the actual audit evidence obtained. The evidence can only be relied upon if it has been obtained appropriately. The engagement partner is therefore looking to ensure that the firm's standards and procedures have been followed in obtaining the evidence.

The engagement performance review itself has five areas, which are summarised below. This is a summary : ISA 220 does have quite a lot of detail – but the headlines here do show the extent of work of the engagement partner.

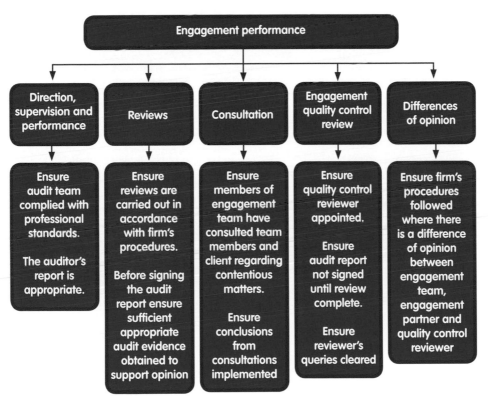

Engagement performance – quality control review

The quality control review, mentioned in the table above, is carried out by a senior member of the audit firm who has not been involved with the audit – ensuring that the reviewer is independent of the evidence being reviewed. This review has two important elements:

Element	Purpose
To ensure that the audit opinion is based on the audit evidence obtained, and	Confirms that the audit opinion is supported by appropriate evidence. As a last resort, the auditor can defend the opinion in court!
To ensure that the audit team was independent of the client and that audit documentation reviewed does actually reflect the work performed.	Confirms that the audit evidence is not biased by independence issues (see chapter 2) so the evidence can be relied on.

Engagement performance - documentation

Finally, the performance review ensures that audit documentation includes:

Documentation includes	Reason for this
Evidence that ethical and independence issues have been considered.	To confirm that the audit firm and the engagement team are independent of the client – and not therefore biased in reaching their opinion.
A quality control review.	To confirm firm's quality control procedures have been followed and there are no unresolved issues from this review.

Audit evidence review

Part of the engagement partner's final review concerns audit evidence; in other words, ensuring that there is sufficient evidence to support the audit opinion.

Each audit firm will have its own checklist for ensuring the audit file is complete. Typical checklist questions will include:

Are the audit strategy and audit plan documented and have these been followed?	✓
Has the work been carried out in accordance with the audit firm's and the profession's standards?	✓
Has the work been carried out in accordance with any legal requirements?	✓
Has the audit team consulted appropriate staff (in the audit firm and at the client) to resolve any queries and problems found on the audit?	✓
Has a memo been produced with points to be considered on next year's audit?	✓
Is there evidence of review at all levels (senior, manager, partner etc)?	✓
Does the audit work support the audit conclusion reached?	✓

8.9 So where are we now?

Almost at the end of the audit. The only thing remaining to do is write the audit report – that is the subject of the next chapter.

8.10 Summary of the summary

Finally the chapter summary; succinct and to the point:

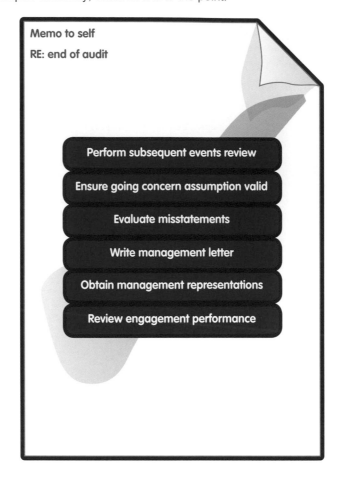

Memo to self

RE: end of audit

Perform subsequent events review

Ensure going concern assumption valid

Evaluate misstatements

Write management letter

Obtain management representations

Review engagement performance

Chapter 9

The audit cycle

reporting

A student's guide to Auditing By Alan Lewin

9.1 Introduction – what will you learn?

This is it – the reason for auditors being in existence – the writing of the audit report. Here we have the auditor reporting back to the shareholders on the results of the audit; did the management really produce financial statements that are accurate and show the results of their stewardship for another year, or are those financial statements defective in some way? All will be revealed in the audit report (assuming that you can understand it in the first place!).

9.2 So, what is in this chapter?

Specifically this chapter explains the different types of audit report that can be produced and when the auditor will produce those reports.

Each of these different reports has an ISA to outline the type of report expected. As in other chapters, that ISA is summarised and where possible explained in plain English terms.

To help navigation through the chapter, here's a summary of the different diversions that an auditor can get on the road to producing a standard unmodified report.

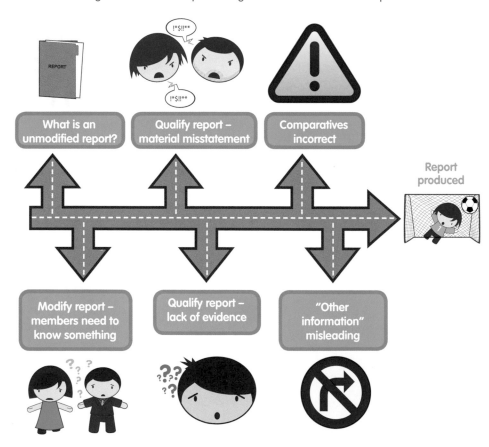

Icon	Event	Chapter reference
	The auditor needs to determine whether sufficient appropriate audit evidence has been obtained to issue a standard or unmodified audit report. These sections explain what a unmodified report is.	9.3 to 9.4
	The auditor finds information that the users of the financial statements need to know about. However, the situation is not so severe that the audit report needs to be qualified.	9.5
	The auditor finds a material misstatement in one or more items in the financial statements. A qualified report will be issued.	9.6 to 9.7
	The auditor believes that all audit evidence has not been made available. Again a qualified report will be issued.	9.8
	The comparative information (prior year's figures in this year's accounts) does not appear to be correct. The auditor must check there is no impact on this year's audit report.	9.9
	Other information issued with the financial statements (such as the CEO's summary of trading for the year) gives a different view of the company when compared to the financial statements. The auditor must try and warn the members of this problem.	9.10
	Goal! The audit report is produced – hopefully "clean" but amended where necessary. The whole chapter is about making this determination.	

9.3 The Unmodified report

An unmodified audit report simply means that the auditor is expressing an opinion without reservation that the financial statements:

- show a true and fair view, and
- have been properly prepared in accordance with the relevant reporting framework.

Auditor's objectives

Issuing the audit report is the most important job of the auditor. This is the document that is available for anyone to read – so the objective of the auditor is to get this report right. Any error will mean not only that the opinion on the financial statements incorrect, but also that the reputation of the auditor may suffer as the audit was not carried out to the correct standard.

However, according to ISA 700, specific objectives that the auditor must follow are:

ISA Statement	Plain English statement
To form an opinion on the financial statements based on an evaluation of the conclusions drawn from the audit evidence obtained.	The auditor will review all the audit evidence collected during the audit, ensuring that there is sufficient evidence to form an opinion on the financial statements of the entity.
To express clearly that opinion through a written report that also describes the basis for that opinion.	The auditor will then state that opinion in a report (paper based or electronic – or both) explaining how that opinion was formed – referring to the method of evidence collection and reliance on ISAs.

In other words, there are two things that the auditor must do:

1. form an opinion, and then

2. express that opinion in a report.

How the auditor forms an opinion

Forming an opinion in general terms may appear to be easy – something is either "right" or "wrong". However, this is not the case with audit opinions. ISA 700 explicitly requires the auditor to make a number of decisions to form the opinion on the financial statements. Remember we are trying to ensure that the financial statements are "true and fair" – only then can the auditor issue the unmodified audit report.

k and d The diagram below summarises the decisions from the ISA into a series of questions. A "yes" answer to all questions means that the unmodified report is issued. Any "no" answers will almost certainly result in a qualified opinion – see sections 9.5 to 9.8 for more detail on qualified opinions.

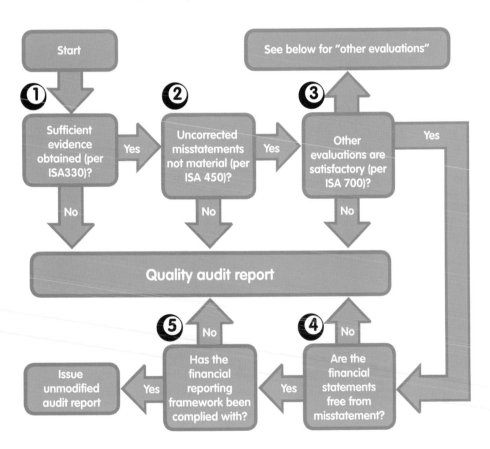

Question	Meaning
①	ISA 330 requires the auditor to obtain sufficient reliable audit evidence. If evidence cannot be obtained then the auditor will normally be uncertain about whether the financial statements are correct – resulting in a qualification.
②	You may recall that the auditor keeps a record of all misstatements found during the audit. In Chapter 8 we considered whether or not these individual small misstatements added up to an overall material misstatement. If they do, then a qualified audit report will be issued.
③	ISA700 refers to "other evaluations" that must be made on the financial statements. The evaluations refer to accounting policies used by the company and disclosure of those policies. Briefly, these evaluations are as follows:

Evaluation	Comment
Are the financial statements prepared in accordance with the financial reporting framework?	The management must have complied with the financial reporting framework used in their country.
Accounting policies, accounting estimates and disclosure are acceptable.	The accounting policies must be right for the company and those policies are explained correctly in the financial statements.
The financial statements fairly present all information?	The auditor must be satisfied that there is no undue emphasis on any item in the financial statements.
The financial statements adequately refer to the financial reporting framework?	The financial reporting framework used (e.g. IFRS) must be clearly stated.
Any "no" answer will result in a qualified audit report.	

Question	Meaning
④	Overall, the financial statements must be free of material misstatement both in terms of disclosure and accuracy of the figures in those financial statements.
⑤	Finally, the financial reporting framework already disclosed must be followed by management – if this is not done then again a qualified report will be issued.

If all these questions are answered "yes" then the auditor can conclude that the financial statements are free from material error and a unmodified audit report can be issued.

The next section explains how to express that standard opinion.

9.4 How to report: Elements of an unmodified audit report

When the auditor concludes that the financial statements are free from material error, the standard audit report can be issued.

This has 10 different sections. Unfortunately if you are taking an auditing exam you do need to learn these. The diagram below shows this unmodified audit report. The different sections are explained in the table below this outline.

 and The good news is that for most auditing exams the detailed wording of the report does not have to be memorised; that can be obtained from the ISA. However, the reasons for the different elements of the report being there does have to be known.

Standard unmodified audit report

Independent auditor's report

Independent auditor's report to the members of 27/4Books Ltd.

Report on the Financial Statements ③

We have audited the accompanying financial statements of 27/4Books Ltd, which comprise the Statement of Financial Position as at December 31, 20X1, and the Income Statement, statement of changes in equity and cash flow statement for the year then ended, and a summary of significant accounting policies and other explanatory information.

Management's Responsibility for the Financial Statements ④

Management is responsible for the preparation and fair presentation of these financial statements in accordance with International Financial Reporting Standards, and for such internal control as management determines is necessary to enable the preparation of financial statements that are free from material misstatement, whether due to fraud or error.

Auditor's Responsibility ⑤

Our responsibility is to express an opinion on these financial statements based on our audit. We conducted our audit in accordance with International Standards on Auditing. Those standards require that we comply with ethical requirements and plan and perform the audit to obtain reasonable assurance about whether the financial statements are free from material misstatement.

An audit involves performing procedures to obtain audit evidence about the amounts and disclosures in the financial statements. The procedures selected depend on the auditor's judgment, including the assessment of the risks of material misstatement of the financial statements, whether due to fraud or error. In making those risk assessments, the auditor considers internal control relevant to the entity's preparation and fair presentation of the financial statements in order to design audit procedures that are appropriate in the circumstances, but not for the purpose of expressing an opinion on the effectiveness of the entity's internal control. An audit also includes evaluating the appropriateness of accounting policies used and the reasonableness of accounting estimates made by management, as well as evaluating the overall presentation of the financial statements.

We believe that the audit evidence we have obtained is sufficient and appropriate to provide a basis for our audit opinion.

Opinion ⑥

In our opinion, the financial statements give a true and fair view of the financial position of 27/4Books Ltd as at December 31, 20X1, and of its financial performance and its cash flows for the year then ended in accordance with International Financial Reporting Standards.

Report on Other Legal and Regulatory Requirements ⑦

[The form and content of this section of the auditor's report will vary depending on the nature of the auditor's other reporting responsibilities.]

SonSmith Auditors LLP, Accountants and auditors ⑧
February 28 20X2 ⑨
London ⑩

Explanation of the unmodified audit report

The elements of an unmodified report are explained below.

Report section	Title	Why is it there?
①	Title	So users know this is the report of an independent auditor.
②	Addressee	To identify who the report is being written to. These are the people who can place reliance on the report.
③	Introductory paragraph	To confirm: 1. which entity is being audited 2. that the financial statements have been audited 3. what the financial statements actually are – normally by stating their titles such as Income Statement and Statement of Financial Position 4. which accounting policies have been used to prepare the financial statements 5. the accounting period covered by the financial statements being audited. In other words the user now knows which parts of a company report have been audited.

Report section	Title	Why is it there?
4	Management's responsibility for financial statements	To let the readers of the financial statements know that it is management who: • are responsible for the preparation of the financial statements (including ensuring compliance with the relevant reporting framework), and • establish the internal control system to ensure that the financial statements are free from material misstatement.
5	Auditor's responsibility	To give information about the work of the auditor in auditing the financial statements. Specifically: • ISAs were used – not just the standards the auditor thought were relevant • the auditor has complied with ethical standards – so the audit was carried out "professionally" • that audit work was planned to try to ensure the financial statements are free from material misstatement – in other words immaterial errors may still be there.
6	Auditor's opinion	The important part of the report – this is the auditor's professional opinion on whether the financial statements give a true and fair view in accordance with the relevant financial reporting framework. The opinion has to be there so users of the financial statements know whether or not those statements are basically "correct".
7	Other reporting responsibilities	Many jurisdictions have other reporting requirements – the auditor must also comply with these. For example, in the United Kingdom there is the requirement to comply with the requirements of the Companies Act 2006.
8	Signature of the auditor	So users know who has actually carried out the audit. The signature is either that of the auditor or the audit firm that the engagement partner works for.

Report section	Title	Why is it there?
⑨	Date of the auditor's report	The date shows when the report was signed. However, the date will be not be earlier than the date the directors sign the financial statements – it is only at this time that the directors formally take responsibility for the financial statements.
⑩	Auditor's address	This is the location – normally the city – where the auditor works – so the auditor can be traced if necessary. For example to resolve a query on the financial statements.

So that's it, the most common form of audit report – the auditor saying that the financial statements are "OK"; any errors are negligible (immaterial) and everything is disclosed about right.

However, we also need to discuss types of audit report which are not standard. To be fair in the real world, there are relatively few of these reports compared to unmodified reports. However, examination questions are almost always based around non-standard reports simply because there are potentially many more questions that can be asked. So again we need to discuss these reports in some detail.

9.5 The "modified" report

Introduction

Where an auditor's report is amended away from the standard unmodified report (explained above) it is said to be "modified".

d There are actually two types of report which are not unmodified reports:

- modified – which are explained in this section, and
- qualified – which are explained in sections 9.6 to 9.8 below.

Briefly, a modified opinion means that the financial statements show a true and fair view but the auditor believes that the users of those financial statements need to be aware of some important matter.

A qualified opinion means that something is "wrong" with the financial statements and the auditor is qualifying the audit report because the financial statements are not correct in some way. These reports are explained in section 9.6 onwards.

Auditor's objectives

At the end of an audit, as we have already seen above, the auditor must decide on the type of report to issue. There are some situations where the auditor wants to bring some matter to the attention of users of the financial statements, but the situations do not warrant amending the opinion of the auditor. The auditor therefore "draws attention" to these matters by including an additional statement in the audit report.

The specific objectives from ISA 706 that the auditor must follow are:

d ISA Statement	Plain English statement
The objective of the auditor, having formed an opinion on the financial statements, is to draw users' attention, when in the auditor's judgment it is necessary to do so, by way of clear additional communication in the auditor's report, to:	The auditor may need to let the users of the financial statements know other information by including some statement in the auditor's report.
(a) a matter, although appropriately presented or disclosed in the financial statements, that is of such importance that it is fundamental to users' understanding of the financial statements, or	That statement may refer to information already in the financial statements that the users must be aware of, or
(b) as appropriate, any other matter that is relevant to users' understanding of the audit, the auditor's responsibilities or the auditor's report.	other things affecting the auditor or the auditor's ability to report.

In other words there are two types of modified report:

1. emphasis of matter, which refers specifically to matters in the financial statements, and

2. other matters, which refer to anything else that the auditor may wish to bring to the attention of the users of the financial statements.

The distinction may be subtle, but the two reports are explained in more detail below.

Types of modified reports

The following table shows the differences between "emphasis of matter" and "other matter" modified audit reports.

Question	Emphasis of matter	Other matter
What is this?	The auditor drawing attention to some information in the financial statements that is considered "fundamental" to the users' understanding of the financial statements.	Additional information about the auditor's responsibilities that the auditor believes the users of the financial statements need to know about.
Where does the paragraph go in the audit report?	After the opinion paragraph and before the auditor's signature.	After the opinion paragraph. AND any emphasis of matter paragraph.
How does the user identify this paragraph?	It has the heading "Emphasis of matter".	It has the heading "Other matter".
What key point does the paragraph include?	A reference to the matter which the auditor wishes to draw attention to in the financial statements (by way of financial statements note number or page number).	The effect on the auditor's responsibilities.
How is the auditor's opinion affected by the statement?	It isn't and a note stating that the auditor's opinion is not amended is included in the emphasis of matter.	It isn't although unlike emphasis of matter the ISA does not specifically state that a note confirming that the opinion is unchanged is required in respect of Other Matter.
Can you give me any examples of these amendments?	Yes, these include: • uncertainties regarding the outcome of litigation • early application of a new accounting standard (that is before the standard's start date) where the financial statements are significantly affected by applying that standard • a major disaster which continues to affect the company.	Yes, these include: • in some jurisdictions, providing additional details on the auditor's responsibilities • in some situations, where the auditor would like to resign, but cannot (but sorry no examples available – the ISA simply states this is a possibility).

Question	Emphasis of matter	Other matter
Do any ISAs specifically require these amendments?	Yes, see for example [1]: ISA 210, Agreeing the Terms of Audit Engagements (Legal financial reporting framework not relevant for client). ISA 560, Subsequent Events – various disclosures on subsequent events. ISA 570, Going Concern – disclosure of going concern concept. ISA 800, (not covered in this book).	Yes, see for example [1]: ISA 560, Subsequent Events, paragraphs various disclosures regarding subsequent events. ISA 710, Comparative Information—Corresponding Figures and Comparative Financial Statements – prior year figures audited by another auditor or not audited at all. ISA 720, The Auditor's Responsibilities Relating to Other Information in Documents Containing Audited Financial Statements - revision of other information is necessary.

[1] For exact ISA references see Appendices 1 and 2 in ISA 706

So there you have it; two ways of amending an unmodified audit report without actually qualifying it.

Example of emphasis of matter

The most common emphasis of matter paragraph relates to lawsuits.

For example, in 27/4Books, an employee may have been injured at work and sue the company for not providing safe working conditions. A forklift truck may have run over the employee's foot. In this situation, the directors may decide to place a note in the financial statements of 27/4Books explaining that litigation is ongoing in respect of this matter, but that no liability is expected.

The auditor will draw attention to this matter in the audit report, simply because potential liability could be quite large; adversely affecting 27/4Books. The standard working used in this case is:

Emphasis of Matter

We draw attention to Note X to the financial statements which describes the uncertainty relating to the outcome of the lawsuit filed against the company by an employee. Our opinion is not qualified in respect of this matter.

Notice that the extract meets the requirements of the ISA because it:

1. appears immediately after the opinion paragraph

2. is headed "emphasis of matter"

3. draws attention to something in the financial statements (Note X), and

4. states that the auditor's opinion is not qualified in respect of this matter.

9.6 The "qualified" report

Introduction

A qualified audit report means that the auditor has reservations about some aspect or aspects of the financial statements. The report is qualified to draw users' attention to those problems.

To help users understand qualifications, the relevant ISA (in this case 705 *Modifications to the opinion in the independent auditor's report*) recommends standard wording to be used. Of course, this assumes you have read the ISA in the first place so you can understand the code...

Auditor's objectives

The auditor's objective in qualifying the audit report is to ensure that the qualification is firstly correct and then secondly understandable by the users of the financial statements. Or as the ISA says:

ISA Statement	Plain English statement
The objective of the auditor is to express clearly an appropriately modified opinion on the financial statements that is necessary when:	The auditor must modify the audit report, that is amend the report from the standard unmodified report when:
(a) The auditor concludes, based on the audit evidence obtained, that the financial statements as a whole are not free from material misstatement; or	there is evidence to suggest that the financial statements contain material error(s), or
(b) The auditor is unable to obtain sufficient appropriate audit evidence to conclude that the financial statements as a whole are free from material misstatement.	there is insufficient evidence to confirm that the financial statements do not contain material error(s).

This means that there are two possible types of qualification:

1. situations where the auditor has all the audit evidence required and can form an opinion that the financial statements are incorrect, and

2. situations where the auditor has not been able to obtain the evidence needed and so cannot confirm that the financial statements are correct.

The ISA also explains that the type of qualification depends on how serious the material misstatement or lack of evidence actually is. There are two possibilities:

1. the material misstatement or lack of evidence gives rise to a material but not pervasive effect on the financial statements, or

2. the material misstatement or lack of evidence gives rise to a material and pervasive effect on the financial statements.

The difference between material but not pervasive and material and pervasive is one of how bad the effect on the financial statements is. This will be explained in the sections below.

For now, here is a decision tree to help you decide on the type of audit opinion required.

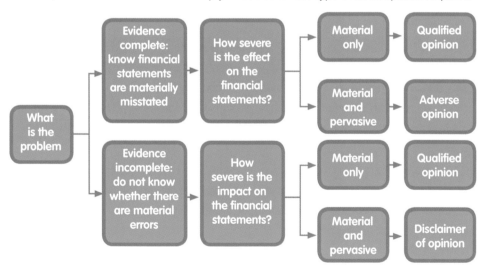

In other words, to decide on the appropriate form of qualification, there are two key questions to answer:

1. what is the problem (answer: either evidence collection complete and there is a material misstatement OR evidence collection incomplete)

2. how severe is the problem (answer: either material only OR material and pervasive).

Answer those questions and you get the type of audit opinion required. Section 9.7 below explains audit reports where all evidence has been obtained and section 9.8 where all the necessary audit evidence is not available.

9.7 Qualified reports – all audit evidence available

Effect on the audit report

In this situation, the auditor knows that something is wrong – sufficient audit evidence has been collected and the auditor does not agree with either the amount of some assets or liabilities or the extent of disclosure of those assets/liabilities. So the auditor needs to tell the users of the financial statements of this problem.

k and **d** But, to summarise first; in this situation the material misstatement, that is the error that the auditor has found in the financial statements, may not simply be that an amount in the financial statements is incorrect. ISA705 provides three situations where the auditor can disagree with the financial statements:

Material misstatement relates to (per ISA705):	Example	Auditor's action
Amounts in the financial statements.	Inventory has been valued at cost rather than lower of cost and net realisable value so the value of inventory is over-stated.	Describe and quantify the effects of the misstatement – that is state how much inventory is overvalued by.
Narrative disclosures in the financial statements.	The accounting policy regarding inventory states the valuation method is lower of cost and net realisable value when valuation was actually based on cost only.	Explain how the disclosure is incorrect – that is state what the disclosure should have been.
Non-disclosure of information that is required to be disclosed in the financial statements.	Information concerning transactions with directors (such as loans to directors from the company) is not provided.	Include the information that has been omitted (unless prohibited by law) – that is state the amount of the loans.

The auditor will need to draw attention to these problems in what is called the "Basis for qualified opinion" paragraph. This is an additional paragraph in an audit report placed after the *Auditor's responsibilities* paragraph and before the *opinion* paragraph. This new paragraph is a warning to the user of the financial statements that something is wrong.

The basis for qualified opinion paragraph

Following a basis for qualified paragraph in an audit report, the opinion paragraph also needs amendment to show the effect of the auditor's understanding of the material misstatement on the audit opinion.

There are two possible amendments depending on the severity of the situation. As noted above, the situation can either be material or material and pervasive. A material situation gives rise to a (well) material qualification, and a material and pervasive situation results in an adverse qualification, as summarised below:

Type of qualification	Auditor states that	In other words:
Material	Except for the effects of the matter(s) described in the Basis for Qualified Opinion paragraph, the financial statements give a true and fair view in accordance with the applicable financial reporting framework.	The auditor is stating that the financial statements are materially correct except for this one item.
Adverse	Because of the significance of the matter(s) described in the Basis for Adverse Opinion paragraph, the financial statements do not give a true and fair view in accordance with the applicable financial reporting framework.	The auditor is stating that because the matter or matters explained in the audit report are so significant the financial statements have been prepared incorrectly.

Audit report examples

We'll now work through the two audit report qualifications that are relevant to situations where the auditor has the evidence required, as explained above. Each report is explained as follows:

1. example from 27/4Books including the two questions to form the correct opinion

2. explanation of the effect of that opinion on the audit report, and

3. example of the opinion showing the changes from the standard opinion.

Audit reports for situations where the auditor lacks evidence are discussed in section 9.8.

Opinion 1 – all evidence obtained – material misstatement

Example from 27/4 books

In this situation, the auditor has obtained all the evidence required but reaches a conclusion that something in the financial statements is incorrect.

In 27/4Books, the management have decided to value inventory at cost only, not the lower of cost and net realisable value. This means that some books will be overvalued as their realisable value will be less than cost.

If this over-valuation is material, then the auditor will issue a material qualification. The rationale for this is (using our qualification questions from section 9.6):

1. what is the problem : "I know that inventory is over-valued"

2. how severe is the problem : "the over-valuation is material to inventory but the rest of the financial statements are OK. The problem is therefore material to inventory but not pervasive to the financial statements as a whole".

Conclusion – this is a material qualification.

Effect on the audit report

The effects on the audit report for this qualification are shown below. The auditor's responsibility paragraph is not changed as all the audit evidence that could be obtained has been obtained. However, a Basis for Qualified Opinion paragraph is added to the report and the Opinion paragraph is amended to show the effect of the incorrect inventory valuation on the auditor's opinion.

In summary, the auditor's report is amended as follows:

Auditor's responsibility	Basis for qualified opinion	Opinion
The paragraph confirms that the auditor has obtained sufficient and appropriate audit evidence to form an opinion.	This is a new paragraph explaining that a qualified opinion is given because inventory is incorrectly valued.	This is now a qualified opinion; the financial statements are correct "except for" the inventory valuation.

Amended audit report

The audit report now reads as follows:

Basis for Qualified Opinion

The company's inventories are carried in the Statement of Financial Position at xxx. Management has not stated the inventories at the lower of cost and net realisable value but has stated them solely at cost, which constitutes a departure from International Financial Reporting Standards. The company's records indicate that had management stated the inventories at the lower of cost and net realisable value, an amount of xxx would have been required to write the inventories down to their net realisable value. Accordingly, cost of sales would have been increased by xxx, and income tax, net income and shareholders' equity would have been reduced by xxx, xxx and xxx, respectively.

Incorrect valuation method

Amount of adjustment

Effect on financial statements balances

Qualified Opinion

In our opinion, except for the effects of the matter described in the Basis for Qualified Opinion paragraph, the financial statements give a true and fair view of the financial position of 27/4 Books as at December 31, 20X1, of its financial performance and its cash flows for the year then ended in accordance with International Financial Reporting Standards.

Qualification wording

So from this wording you now know that the auditor collected the all the evidence possible but the auditor disagreed with one item of the financial statements causing a material error. Obviously, in a "real" report, the xxx's would be replaced by the appropriate figures.

Opinion 2 – all evidence obtained – material and pervasive qualification

 Example from 27/4Books

In this situation, the auditor has been able to obtain all the evidence required and reaches a conclusion that some matter in the financial statements is so incorrect that it affects the whole of the financial statements.

Let's assume that 27/4Books purchased a subsidiary during the year to 31 December 20X1, but included this subsidiary in the financial statements at cost rather than including the assets at fair value in accordance with accounting standards. This means that the financial statements of 27/4Books are incorrect as the value of the subsidiary is considerably under-stated. Let's assume here that the asset values of 27/4Books would be doubled – that's quite an understatement.

As this under-valuation is significant and affects the financial statements as a whole, then the auditor will issue an adverse qualification. The rationale for this is (using our qualification questions from section 9.6):

1. what is the problem : "27/4Books new subsidiary should have been consolidated"

2. how severe is the problem : "Appears very severe, the new subsidiary effectively doubles the size of 27/4Books – so not showing the subsidiary understates by a very material amount the size of the company".

Conclusion – this is a material and pervasive qualification.

Effect on the audit report

The effects on the audit report for this qualification are shown below. The auditor's responsibility paragraph is not changed as all the audit evidence that could be obtained has been obtained. However, a Basis of Opinion paragraph is added to the report and the Opinion paragraph is amended to show the effect of the incorrect consolidation method.

In summary, the auditor's report is amended as follows:

Auditor's responsibility	Basis for adverse opinion	Opinion
The paragraph confirms that the auditor has obtained sufficient and appropriate audit evidence to form an opinion.	This is now an adverse opinion because the non-consolidation is so significant it affects the whole financial statements.	This is now an adverse opinion; the financial statements do not show a true and fair view because of the significance of the non-consolidation.

Amended audit report

The audit report now reads as follows:

Basis for Adverse Opinion

As explained in Note 12, 27/4Books has not consolidated the financial statements of subsidiary JM Company it acquired during 20X1 because it has not yet been able to ascertain the fair values of certain of the subsidiary's material assets and liabilities at the acquisition date. This investment is therefore accounted for on a cost basis. Under International Financial Reporting Standards, the subsidiary should have been consolidated because it is controlled by the company. Had JM been consolidated, many elements in the accompanying financial statements would have been materially affected. The effects on the consolidated financial statements of the failure to consolidate have not been determined.

Problem in financial statements

Reason for problem in against IFRS

Effect on financial statements balances

Adverse Opinion

In our opinion, because of the significance of the matter discussed in the Basis for Adverse Opinion paragraph, the consolidated financial statements do not give a true and fair view of the financial position of 27/4 Books and its subsidiaries as at December 31, 20X1, and of their financial performance and their cash flows for the year then ended in accordance with International Financial Reporting Standards.

Qualification wording

In other words you now know that the auditor was so concerned about the valuation of the subsidiary that the auditor's opinion is that the financial statements do not give a true and fair view.

9.8 Qualified reports – lack of evidence

Effect on the audit report d

In this situation, the auditor knows that something is wrong – but cannot obtain the audit evidence required to obtain a full understanding of that problem; the evidence is either missing or management may decide to withhold evidence.

and ISA705 recognises three situations where the auditor may not be able to obtain the necessary audit evidence. These situations are summarised below along with examples and appropriate actions for the auditor:

Reason for lack of evidence	Example	Auditor's action
Circumstances beyond the control of the entity	The company's accounting records have been destroyed or government have seized the entities accounting records.	Complete the audit as far as possible and then produce an audit report; probably with a qualification.
Circumstances relating to the nature or timing of audit work	The company has to use an accounting method (by country law) that is not appropriate for the entity, or The auditor is appointed after the year end meaning that attendance at the inventory count is impossible.	Complete the audit as far as possible and then produce an audit report; probably with a qualification.
Limitations imposed by management	Management prevent the auditor from obtaining evidence (e.g. do not allow the auditor to attend the inventory count or obtain necessary third party evidence in a circularisation).	See below for appropriate actions.

As with the situation where the auditor finds a material misstatement in items in the financial statements, the auditor will need to draw attention to these problems in what is called the "Basis for Qualified Opinion" paragraph.

Also, as with the material misstatement situation, there are two possible audit qualifications (although two reasons for using disclaimer of opinion):

d Type of qualification	Situation per ISA 705	In plain English
Material	The auditor is unable to obtain sufficient appropriate audit evidence on which to base the opinion, but the auditor concludes that the possible effects on the financial statements of undetected misstatements, if any, could be material but not pervasive.	The auditor has been prevented (deliberately or not) from obtaining evidence necessary for the audit but believes that the lack of evidence results in material misstatements only.
Disclaimer	The auditor shall disclaim an opinion when the auditor is unable to obtain sufficient appropriate audit evidence on which to base the opinion, and the auditor concludes that the possible effects on the financial statements of undetected misstatements, if any, could be both material and pervasive.	The auditor has been prevented (deliberately or not) from obtaining evidence necessary for the audit but believes that the lack of evidence now results in material and pervasive misstatements hence cannot form an opinion on whether the financial statements are correct.
Disclaimer	The auditor shall disclaim an opinion when, in extremely rare circumstances involving multiple uncertainties, the auditor concludes that, notwithstanding having obtained sufficient appropriate audit evidence regarding each of the individual uncertainties, it is not possible to form an opinion on the financial statements due to the potential interaction of the uncertainties and their possible cumulative effect on the financial statements.	The auditor has obtained sufficient audit evidence, but because there are many uncertainties an overall opinion on the financial statements cannot be given.

A note on management imposed limitation

In the rare situation where management do not co-operate with the auditor, then the auditor will be unable to obtain sufficient appropriate audit evidence to form an opinion. This is concerning because in many countries, management are required to assist the auditor. However, if management will not assist then the auditor must consider what to do next.

The flowchart below shows the decisions and actions that the auditor must take.

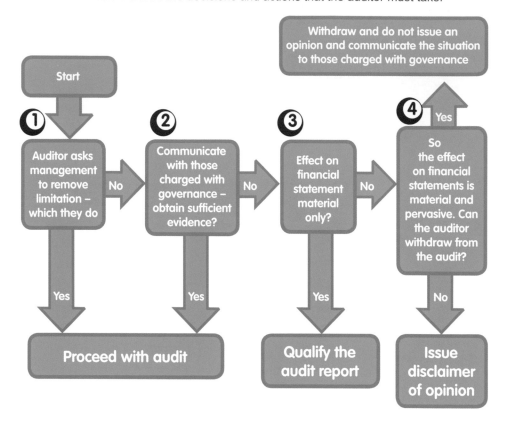

Point	Comment
and	Although the auditor can now proceed with the audit, this will probably be with "professional scepticism" – management are less likely to be trusted given the problems they have already given to the auditor.
	The qualification here will be material.

If the situation is very bad, then the auditor can no longer really work for the shareholders – information is simply not available from management. Withdrawal or resignation from the audit is the only option.

However, if resignation is not possible (perhaps due to legal reasons in that particular country) then a disclaimer opinion is appropriate.

Opinion 3 – lack of evidence – material misstatement

 ## Example from 27/4Books

In this situation, the auditor has not been able to obtain sufficient appropriate audit evidence, and is therefore unsure whether an item on the Statement of Financial Position is correct.

Let's assume that in 27/4Books management informed the auditor after the year end that 30% of the book inventory was now being kept in a third party warehouse and was not included in any computerised inventory systems at 27/4Books main depot. However, the books were included in the inventory balance in the financial statements. This inventory related to books which were due to be published in the next four months and so the books were not available for sale at the year end. As the auditor was only informed of this inventory after the year end, it was not possible to determine existence by physically counting the inventory (the normal audit procedure for existence). Alternative evidence such as a statement from a third party that the inventory exists was also not available.

If this over-valuation is material, then the auditor will issue a material qualification. The rationale for this is (using our qualification questions from section 9.6):

1. what is the problem : "I don't have sufficient audit evidence to determine the existence of inventory in the third party warehouse"

2. how severe is the problem : "the lack of information relates to inventory – and only 30% of the inventory – no other items are affected".

Conclusion – this is a material qualification.

Effect on the audit report

The effects on the audit report for this qualification are shown below. The auditor's responsibility paragraph is amended as all the auditor has not been able to obtain all the evidence necessary for the audit. However, a Basis for Qualified Opinion paragraph is added to the report and the Opinion paragraph is amended to show the effect of the lack of evidence regarding inventory.

In summary, the auditor's report is amended as follows:

Auditor's responsibility	Basis for qualified opinion	Opinion
Amended to state although ISA's were used in conducting the audit, all audit evidence required could not be obtained.	This is now a qualified opinion because of the lack of evidence regarding the existence of part of 27/4Books' inventory	This is now a qualified opinion; the financial statements are correct "except for" the lack of evidence regarding the inventory.

Amended audit report

The audit report now reads as follows:

Auditor's Responsibility

Our responsibility is to express an opinion on these financial statements based on conducting the audit in accordance with International Standards on Auditing. Because of the matter described in the Basis for Qualified Opinion paragraph, however, we were not able to obtain sufficient appropriate audit evidence to provide a basis for an audit opinion.

Lack of audit evidence

Basis for Qualified Opinion

27/4Books maintains a significant amount of inventory in a third party warehouse. The inventory is stated at xxx on the statement of financial position as at December 31, 20X1. We were unable to obtain sufficient appropriate audit evidence about the existence of this inventory as at December 31, 20X1 because we were not aware of the inventory prior to the year-end and third party confirmation was not available. Consequently, we were unable to determine whether any adjustments to reflect lack of existence or valuation were necessary.

Inventory uncertainty relates to

Auditor could not obtain evidence

Uncertainty regarding adjustment needed

Qualified Opinion

In our opinion, except for the possible effects of the matter described in the Basis for Qualified Opinion paragraph, the financial statements give a true and fair view of the financial position of 27/4 Books as at December 31, 20X1, and of its financial performance and its cash flows for the year then ended in accordance with International Financial Reporting Standards.

Qualification wording

So you now know that the auditor could not obtain evidence about one item (the inventory) but that this lack of evidence was only material and not pervasive to the whole financial statements.

Opinion 4 – lack of evidence – material and pervasive qualification

 Example from 27/4Books

In this situation, the auditor has not been able to obtain all the evidence required and reaches a conclusion there is insufficient evidence to reach an opinion on the financial statements as a whole.

Let's assume that in 27/4Books the management have made an investment with another company (called DCL) in country X. This "joint venture" will be to distribute books in country X. However, management refuse to give the auditor any more information about this joint venture (OK this is unusual but the situation has to be really bad for the material and pervasive qualification). As the joint-venture is worth 75% of the assets of 27/4Books, the auditor cannot obtain evidence on a significant amount of the assets of 27/4Books. Key assertions like the valuation of the joint-venture and even its existence cannot be confirmed. This means that the auditor is now unsure whether or not the financial statements are correct; and the evidence to make this decision cannot be obtained.

As this uncertainty affects the whole financial statements, the auditor will issue a disclaimer of opinion. The rationale for this is (using our qualification questions from section 9.6):

1. what is the problem : "I know 27/4Books have a joint-venture with company DCL in country X but I cannot obtain information about this joint-venture"

2. how severe is the problem : "the joint-venture appears to be worth 75% of the value of the assets of 27/4Books – but I cannot confirm this. 75% is a significant amount to get wrong so I really cannot form an opinion on the financial statements as a whole."

Conclusion – this is a material and pervasive qualification.

Effect on the audit report

The effects on the audit report for this qualification are shown below. The auditor's responsibility paragraph is changed as audit evidence could be obtained to resolve the situation but management have taken the decision not to give this to the auditor. A Basis of Disclaimer of Opinion paragraph is added to the report and the Opinion paragraph is amended to show the effect of the lack of evidence regarding the joint-venture.

In summary, the auditor's report is amended as follows:

Auditor's responsibility	Basis for disclaimer of opinion	Opinion
Amended to state although ISAs were used in conducting the audit, all audit evidence required could not be obtained.	This is now a disclaimer of opinion because of lack of evidence on the joint-venture.	This is now a disclaimer of opinion; the auditor cannot determine whether or not the financial statements show a true and fair view.

Amended audit report

The audit report now reads as follows:

Auditor's Responsibility

Our responsibility is to express an opinion on these financial statements based on conducting the audit in accordance with International Standards on Auditing. Because of the matter described in the Basis for Disclaimer of Opinion paragraph, however, we were not able to obtain sufficient appropriate audit evidence to provide a basis for an audit opinion.

Lack of audit evidence

Basis for Disclaimer of Opinion

The company's investment in its joint venture DCL Company is carried at xxx on the company's statement of financial position, which represents over 75% of the company's net assets as at December 31, 20X1. We were not allowed access to the management and the auditors of DCL, including DCL's auditors' audit documentation. As a result, we were unable to determine whether any adjustments were necessary in respect of the company's proportional share of DCL's assets that it controls jointly, its proportional share of DCL's liabilities for which it is jointly responsible, its proportional share of DCL's income and expenses for the year, and the elements making up the statement of changes in equity and cash flow statement.

Reason for lack of evidence

Effect on financial statements balances

Disclaimer of Opinion

Because of the significance of the matter described in the Basis for Disclaimer of Opinion paragraph, we have not been able to obtain sufficient appropriate audit evidence to provide a basis for an audit opinion. Accordingly, we do not express an opinion on the financial statements.

In other words, you now know that management refused to give the auditor information and that this lack of information was material and pervasive to the financial statements so that the auditor cannot express an opinion.

9.9 Comparative information in financial statements

The problem

As you know (or will have seen from the extracts of 27/4Books' financial statements included in this book), financial statements have two year's worth of figures – the year under audit and the previous year. The previous year's figures are technically referred to as "comparative information" and "corresponding figures" because under the same headings of inventory, receivables etc the amount of those balances from last year are shown.

There is a major problem with this comparative information. You have also seen that the audit report only refers to the current year's figures; in other words the comparative information is not audited this year. While this may not be a significant problem for the auditor, there may still be situations where the comparative information affects this year's audit, and the auditor will need to tell the users of the financial statements about this problem.

This section explains when the auditor may need to make reference to comparative figures. The section is relatively brief as there are normally few problems with comparative amounts.

Auditor's objectives

The auditing of comparative information is explained in ISA 710 *Comparative information – corresponding figures and comparative financial statements*. The ISA states clearly that the auditor must obtain information about comparative amounts, even though those amounts are not being specifically audited this year.

Specifically the ISA states that the auditor must:

ISA Statement	Plain English statement
Obtain sufficient appropriate audit evidence about whether the comparative information included in the financial statements has been presented, in all material respects, in accordance with the requirements for comparative information in the applicable financial reporting framework.	The comparative information must be materially correct and the auditor needs to obtain sufficient evidence to confirm this is the case.
Report in accordance with the auditor's reporting responsibilities.	Where there is a need to report to the users problems with the comparative figures then the auditor must do this.

The ISA applies to comparative information and normally refers to situations where that information is not specifically audited. In a minority of situations comparative information is audited and the auditor's report will therefore specifically relate to that comparative information.

Audit procedures – comparative information

Audit procedures on comparative information are limited to:

1. ensuring that the comparative information is the same as that published last year; in other words the audited balances last year should be the same as the comparatives this year – by definition they are the same figures!

2. any changes or restatement of comparatives has been carried out correctly – for example a change of accounting policy has been correctly applied to the comparative figures.

There are a limited number of situations where the auditor may need to mention comparative figures in the audit report; these are outlined below:

Comparative figures – effects on audit report

There are four situations where the auditor will need to amend the audit opinion on this year's financial statements for issues with comparative figures. These situations and corresponding actions are:

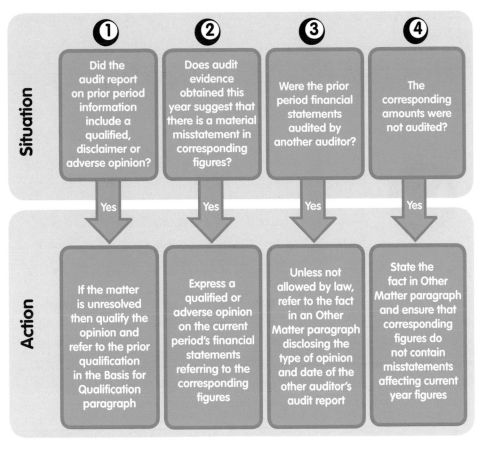

Situation	Comment
①	Audit report qualifications may affect this year's audit opinion. Examples include: Legal claims not being resolved, so there is uncertainty about amounts the company may have to pay. Qualification on inventories; if the opening inventory figure is incorrect then profit for this year will almost certainly be incorrect.
②	Audit work this year suggests misstatements last year. Note that the auditor does not re-audit the comparative figures but simply refers to the effect on this year's audited figures.
③	This is a rare situation where the auditor does refer to the work of other professionals in the audit report. The Other Matter paragraph means this is for information only and is not a limitation in the scope of the work this year.
④	This is closest that the auditor gets to auditing comparative amounts. The auditor may attempt to obtain audit evidence about these amounts. Remember that if sufficient evidence is not obtained then situation 2 above applies and a qualified opinion may be needed.

ISA710 does give examples of the different audit reports on comparative amounts if you are interested.

9.10 Other information issued with audited financial statements

The problem

As you probably know, audited financial statements are normally issued as part of a larger document called the "Annual Report" or something similar. This means that users of financial statements are presented not only with the audited financial statements, but also a lot of "other information" including the chairman's report, the CEO's review of the company etc.

Furthermore, the Annual Report is normally formatted to have all the company review etc at the front, with the financial statements at the end. Users are even tempted to read the first sections due to the use of better quality paper, colour pictures and large writing compared to the financial statements which appear on grey paper with small writing (do have a look at a set of company financial statements and see for yourself!).

The problem is of course that this "other information" is not audited, but is read first (that's assuming that users actually get through to reading the financial statements). What if this other information was incorrect or contradicted the financial statements? Users may not realise there is a problem and believe the other information rather than read the financial statements to get a "true and fair" picture of the company.

To ensure that users are not misled by incorrect "other information", the auditor needs to do something. The next problem is that the auditor has no responsibility for this other information – it is not audited. So even if something was wrong, it will be difficult to tell the users about this. To be fair, most managers are honest and won't try and mislead, but in a minority of situations, especially where company results are poor, there could be a temptation to mislead.

This section explains what work the auditor can do on other information and actions that can be taken to warn users that other information may be incorrect or misleading.

Auditor's objectives

The auditing of "other information" is explained in ISA 720 *The auditor's responsibilities relating to other information in documents containing audited financial statements*. The ISA states clearly that the auditor must read other information issued with financial statements and where inconsistencies are identified, take appropriate action.

Specifically the ISA states that:

d ISA Statement	Plain English statement
The objective of the auditor is to respond appropriately when documents containing audited financial statements and the auditor's report thereon include other information that could undermine the credibility of those financial statements and the auditor's report.	Where other information issued with audited financial information presents a different view of the company (for example, a loss is really a profit) then the auditor needs to tell the users of this problem in some way.

The ISA applies to any other information issued with the financial statements. Two possible circumstances are noted in the ISA regarding other information:

Situation	Explanation	ⓔ Example from 27/4Books
Inconsistencies	This is where other information actually contradicts information in the financial statements.	Management state that 27/4Books has made a profit of $X when the actual profit is $Y.
Misstatements of fact	Here, the other information is not mentioned in the financial statements so there can be no inconsistency with those statements. However, the information is still incorrect.	Management state that 75% of old unsold books have been recycled in accordance with the company's recycling policy. This policy is not audited or mentioned in the financial statements so there is no inconsistency – the information is simply "wrong".

The auditor is mainly concerned with inconsistencies as these undermine the information provided in the financial statements. Audit procedures regarding inconsistencies are explained below.

Misstatements of fact are still important but to some extent less so as the financial statements are not affected. Audit procedures are normally limited to asking management to amend the fact – seeking advice from experts. The auditor may also seek legal expert advice but no other actions are recommended by the ISA.

Audit procedures - inconsistent "Other information"

ISA 720 outlines various problems and actions that the auditor may encounter with inconsistent "other information" in the financial statements. The flowchart below summarises these situations to show the actions that the auditor may take.

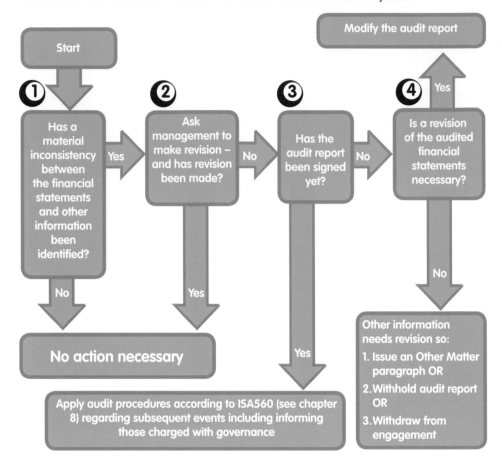

Decision	Comment
①	If the "other information" and the audited information are consistent then no other action is needed; the financial statements and other information agree with each other.
②	As usual, if amendments to the other information or the financial statements need to be made – ask management to do this. The timing here is assumed to be before the audit report is signed so there is still time to amend other information and the financial statements. If amendments are satisfactory then no other action is needed.
③	However, if amendments are needed and the audit report has been signed, then things become a little more difficult. If the financial statements are incorrect, then the same situation applies as with events after the balance sheet date- see chapter 8.3 for detail of the auditor's actions.
④	Finally, if an amendment is required, management won't make the amendment and the audit report has not been signed, then the auditor can still modify the report with a qualification; this action will be taken where the financial statements contain material misstatements.
	However, where the other information contains material misstatements, there is little that the auditor can do; the auditor cannot force management to amend the other information as it is not audited. However, possible actions are shown on the flowchart leading up to resignation as a last resort. Remember on resigning the auditor can require the directors to convene a General Meeting (in some countries) so the members can be told of problems affecting the audit.

9.11 So where are we now?

 Finished! Complete! At the end of the audit! Time to invoice the client, have a celebratory meal (not paid for by the client due to independence issues of course) and move onto the next job.

Or if you are studying for an exam, move onto chapter 10 to remind yourself of all those lovely bits of the ISAs that you must know. If you are not studying, at least join me again at the end of chapter 10 for the final closing remarks. Thank you.

9.12 Summary of the summary

Finally the chapter summary; showing you how to form an audit opinion:

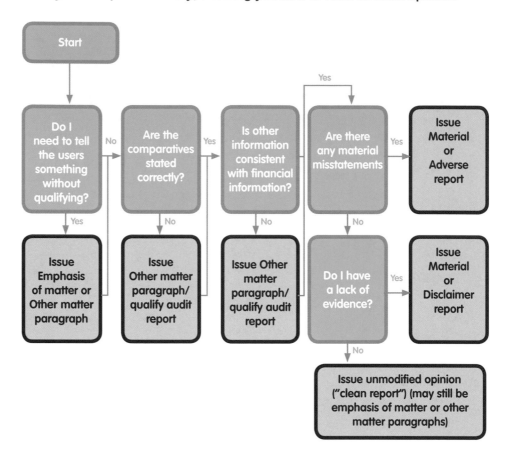

Chapter 10
Revision

Introduction to this chapter

This chapter is designed as a revision aid; but with a small difference. For most of the ISAs and a few other areas, I've asked you a couple of questions about that ISA – and then provided outline answers below each question. You can simply read the question then the answers, or (horrors) cover up the answer, read and try and answer the question before checking the answer. You know that the latter makes sense.

There is a reference back into the earlier chapters for most questions in case you want to remind yourself of the detail again.

The ethical framework

The legal bit

What are the fundamental ethical principles?	What are the main ethical threats that an accountant must guard against?	What powers are given to the auditor to carry out audit work?	What qualifies a person to be an auditor
• Integrity • Objectivity • Professional competence and due care • Confidentiality • Professional behaviour	• Self-interest – conflict between personal interests and client interests. • Self-review – checking your own work. • Advocacy – promoting the client in some way. • Familiarity – being too close or friendly with the client. • Intimidation – client threatens the auditor in some way.	• Access to company's books and records. • Receive all information and explanations auditor considers necessary for audit. • Receive notice of and attend company meetings. • Receive notice of and attend any meeting proposing removal of the auditor. • Upon resignation, right to ask directors to convene a general meeting.	That depends on the individual country, but normally: • Being a member of a professional accountancy institute (an "RSB" in the UK) • Being allowed to audit under the rules of that institute OR • Being authorised separately by the state.
Detail – chapter 2		Detail – chapter 3	

ISA 200 Overall objectives

ISA 210 Engagement letters

What are the overall objectives of an audit?	What are the elements of the audit risk model?	Why do auditors send an engagement letter?	What are the typical contents of an engagement letter?
• Obtain reasonable assurance about whether the financial statements are free from material misstatement. • Report on the financial statements and communicate in accordance with the ISAs.	Audit Risk : Risk that the audit opinion is inappropriate. Inherent Risk : Misstatements due to factors concerning the specific client and the industry client working in. Control Risk : Misstatement not prevented or detected by client's internal control system. Detection Risk : Misstatements not detected by auditor's audit procedures.	• To establish whether the preconditions for an audit are present. • To confirm there is a common understanding between auditor and management and, where appropriate, those charged with governance.	• Confirm scope and objectives of audit. • State responsibilities of auditor. • State responsibilities of management. • Identify the reporting framework. • Confirm basis of fees. • State management representations will be required. • Request management confirm agreement of the letter.
Detail chapter 4.3		Detail chapter 4.4	

ISA 220 – Quality control

ISA 230 Audit documentation

What objectives must an auditor meet to maintain appropriate quality in an audit?	What are the responsibilities of the engagement partner regarding quality control of the audit?	What are the qualities of good audit documentation?	Why does the auditor produce audit documentation?
• Audit must comply with professional standards and appropriate legal and regulatory requirements. • Audit report issued is appropriate for the circumstances of the client company.	• Ensure quality control standards are followed. • Ensure ethical standards are followed. • Maintain independence from client. • Ensure auditor appointed correctly. • Check audit team have sufficient competence. • Review work carried out. • Appoint quality control reviewer.	• Provide sufficient and appropriate record to support auditor's report. • Provide evidence that the audit was planned in accordance with ISA and applicable legal and regulatory requirements.	• Helps plan the audit. • Audit evidence that audit work has been carried out. • Shows who produced what documentation. • Evidence to assist planning future audits. • Shows quality control standards have been followed. • Shows auditor complied with ISAs and any other relevant regulation.
Detail chapters 5.4 and 8.8		Detail chapter 5.10	

ISA 240 Fraud

What are the auditor's responsibilities regarding fraud?	What is the normal audit work regarding fraud?
• Determine whether the financial statements have material misstatements caused by fraud. • Obtain sufficient audit evidence to decide whether material misstatement has occurred due to fraud. • If fraud is found, take appropriate action e.g. report to management.	• Maintain attitude of professional scepticism. • Find out how management assess the risk of fraud. • Assess risk of material misstatement due to fraud. • Evaluate audit evidence obtained. • Communicate concerns to those charged with governance.

Detail chapter 4.9

ISA 265 Management letters

What situations does the auditor report in a management letter?	What does the letter say about each internal control deficiency?
• Controls are designed, implemented or operated in a way that means the control will not prevent or detect / correct a misstatement in the financial statements. • Controls to prevent, detect / correct misstatements in the financial statements are missing.	• Explanation of the deficiency. • Description of the potential effect of the deficiency. • Suggest remedial action to overcome the deficiency.

Detail chapter 8.7

ISA 300 Audit planning

What are the benefits of planning an audit?	What is the audit strategy?	What is the audit risk model?
• Devote attention to appropriate areas of the audit.	Audit strategy is the overall approach to the audit.	Inherent risk
		x
• Identify and resolve problems in a timely manner.	Consists of three elements:	Control risk
• Audit is performed efficiently and effectively.	• audit scope	x
• Select appropriate members for engagement team.	• audit timing	Detection risk
	• audit direction	=
• Assist direction and supervision of audit.	and	
• Co-ordinate work of auditors and experts.	identifies risky areas for attention on audit.	Audit risk
	Detail chapter 4.5 to 4.8	

ISA 315 Identifying and assessing risks

What are the four stages of assessing risk in an audit?	In assessing internal control systems what are the internal control elements?	What are the main control activities that the auditor can place reliance on?	Why can audit procedures give an incorrect result?
• Initial procedures to identify risk e.g. talking to management and analytical procedures. • Obtain information about client and industry; assessing inherent risk. • Obtain information about the client's internal control systems; assessing control risk. • Determine where and whether material misstatement could occur.	• Control environment. • Entity's risk assessment process. • Information systems. • Control activities. • Monitoring of controls. Note these elements may also be referred to as internal control components.	• Performance reviews. • Information processing : application controls. • Information processing : general IT controls. • Physical controls. • Segregation of duties. • Other control activities such as authorisation controls.	• Sampling risk : the sample chosen is not representative of the population. • Non-sampling risk : the auditor applies audit procedures incorrectly.

Detail chapters 4.6 and 4.7

ISA 315 Identifying and assessing risks

ISA 320 Materiality

What are the audit assertions relating to the income statement?	What are the audit assertions relating to the statement of financial position?	What is materiality?	What are the guidelines for materiality?
• Occurrence – transaction occurred and belongs to entity. • Completeness – all transactions recorded. • Accuracy – amounts recorded correctly. • Cut-off – recorded in correct accounting period. • Classification – recorded in correct accounts.	• Existence – item actually exists at the reporting date. • Rights and obligations – entity owns the asset or has obligation to pay a liability. • Completeness – all assets and liabilities recorded. • Valuation and Allocation – assets and liabilities included in financial statements at appropriate amount.	**Materiality** The amount by which a figure in the financial statements must change to influence the economic decisions of users of the financial statements. **Performance materiality** The amount used by the auditor in planning audit procedures – less than materiality itself.	• Profit before tax (5% for a manufacturing company). • Gross profit (no guideline in the ISA). • Turnover (1% for a not-for-profit company). Else use of the auditor's judgement.
Detail chapter 6.3 and 7.5		Detail chapter 5.5	

ISA 330 Response to assessed risks

ISA 450 Evaluation of misstatements

What are the steps the auditor uses to collect evidence regarding an identified risk?	What types of procedures can the auditor use to collect audit evidence?	Why must an auditor evaluate misstatements?	What steps must the auditor take when misstatements are identified?
• Identify the risk.	• Substantive analytical procedures.	• To find the effect of identified misstatements on the audit.	• Keep a record of misstatements found.
• Determine the level of risk of material misstatement.	• Tests of detail.	• To find the effect of uncorrected misstatements on the financial statements.	• Decide whether audit strategy or plan needs revising for misstatements found.
• Decide on the mix of audit procedures to collect evidence.	• Tests of controls.		• Ask management to correct misstatements found.
• Review evidence collected and determine whether a material error has occurred.			• Evaluate effect on financial statements of uncorrected misstatements.
			• Inform management about misstatements.
			• Obtain management representation letter.
			• Consider effect on audit report of unadjusted misstatements.
Detail chapter 5.11 and 5.6		Detail chapter 5.11 and 8.5	

ISA 500 Audit evidence

ISA 505 External confirmations

What types of audit procedure can be used to collect audit evidence?	What are the characteristics of "good" audit evidence?	What are the key points regarding external confirmations?	What examples of external confirmations are in this book?
• Inspection • Observation • External confirmation • Recalculation • Reperformance • Analytical procedures • Inquiry	Audit evidence should be: **Relevant** • To the assertion being tested **Reliable** Guidelines to reliability being: • from independent sources • internal (where good internal control systems) • obtained directly by the auditor • documentary • original documents.	• Good source of evidence (external to client being audited and independent). • Must be sent by auditor and received back to auditor. • Can save time during audit. • Positive confirmation (response requested to all letters) provides more reliable evidence than negative (response requested only when errors found).	• Receivables circularisation (section 7.8). • Payables circularisation (section 7.11). • Bank letter (section 7.13).
	Detail chapter 5.7	Detail – see three references above	

ISA 520 Analytical procedures

ISA 530 Statistical sampling

What are the steps for carrying out effective analytical procedures?	When can the auditor use analytical procedures?	What are the steps for conducting a test using sampling?	What types of sampling method can an auditor use?
• Ensure analytical procedures can be used.	• Start of the audit (part of risk assessment).	• Identify purpose of audit procedure.	• Random (use of random number tables).
• Ensure data to be used in analytical procedures is reliable.	• During the audit (substantive analytical procedures).	• Determine the sample size.	• Systematic (every n^{th} item).
• From this data, form an expectation of figures in the financial statements.	• End of the audit (confirm financial statement figures meet expectations from audit work).	• Select items for testing.	• Monetary unit sampling (sampling unit is $(rather than items in the population)).
• Compare expectation to financial statements – account for any differences found.		• Perform audit procedures on those items.	• Haphazard (auditor uses skill and judgement).
		• Where necessary select alternative items for testing.	• Block (items next to each other e.g. everything in April).
		• Determine reasons for errors found.	
		• Calculate population misstatement.	
		• Evaluate results of testing.	
Detail chapter 5.9 and 7.4			Detail chapter 5.8

ISA 550 Related parties

ISA 560 Subsequent events

What is the standard audit work on related party transactions?	Who are related parties anyway?	What types of subsequent events are there?	What are the auditor's responsibilities regarding subsequent events?
• Try and identify related parties. • Look out for related party transactions during the audit. • Assess risk of misstatement due to related party transactions. • Keep audit team and management informed concerning related party transactions found. • Consider effect of transactions found on audit opinion.	Examples of related parties include: • people or entities having direct or indirect equity holdings in the audited entity • direct or indirect holdings by the company being audited in other entities • member of management or those charged with governance • close family members of 3 above • a significant business relationship with persons in 3 above.	Events after the reporting date either: • provide evidence of conditions that existed at that date (and so financial statements may need adjustment) or • provide evidence of conditions that arose after that date (and so financial statements are not adjusted but disclosure of the event may be needed).	Reporting date to signing of audit report • identify events • ensure financial statements amended as necessary. Audit report to financial statements issued • Ask directors to amend financial statements • Amend audit report. Post financial statements issued • Amend audit report (if directors allow). • Ensure existing report not relied on.
Detail chapter 5.12			Detail chapter 8.3

ISA 570 Going concern

What are the auditor's responsibilities regarding going concern?	What are the normal audit procedures with respect to the going concern assumption?
• Obtain sufficient evidence to confirm management were right to use the going concern assumption to prepare the financial statements. • Conclude whether there is a material uncertainty regarding the use of the going concern assumption. • Determine the implications for the audit report of any uncertainty identified above.	• Ask management to make assessment of company's going concern status. • Review plans showing company should continue trading. • Evaluate cash flow forecasts. • Review any other relevant data. • Obtain management representation point.

Detail chapter 8.4

ISA 580 Management representations

What is the process to obtaining a management representation letter?	What are the normal contents of the management representation letter?
• Auditor decides contents of representation letter. • Auditor prepares letter and sends draft to management. • Management review and sign letter. • Auditor then files letter in working papers as audit evidence.	Contents required by ISA • management confirm financial statements prepared in accordance with applicable financial reporting framework • management provided auditor with all information and explanations required for audit • management confirm all transactions recorded in financial statements. Other contents can include: • details of liabilities • confirmation of going concern status • valuation of investments etc.

Detail chapter 8.6

ISA 610 Internal audit

ISA 620 Reliance on experts

Is the work of internal audit adequate?	Is internal audit work of sufficient standard?	How does the auditor decide that the expert is competent, capable and objective?	How does the auditor evaluate the work produced by the expert?
Review internal auditor's: • objectivity • technical competence • due professional care.	Check: • staff have sufficient training • staff properly supervised • sufficient evidence obtained to support conclusions reached • final report based on those conclusions • problems found have been resolved.	Obtaining evidence such as: • personal knowledge of expert • recommendations from other auditors • expert has appropriate professional qualification • published work of the expert.	By: • comparing to other audit evidence obtained • ensuring assumptions and conclusions of expert are reasonable • ensuring data used by expert is complete and accurate.
Detail chapter 3.10 and 5.13		Detail chapter 5.14	

ISA 700 Independent auditor's report – ISA 705 Modified / qualified auditor's reports

What must the auditor report on?	What are the elements of an unmodified audit report?	On what grounds is an audit report qualified?	How does the audit report change depending on the seriousness of the situation?
• Whether the financial statements present fairly (or show a true and fair view) the financial position of the entity. • The financial statements have been prepared in accordance with the applicable financial reporting framework. • Any other matters prescribed by statute.	• Title • Addressee • Introductory paragraph • Management's responsibility for the financial statements • Auditor's responsibility • Auditor's opinion • Other reporting responsibilities • Signature of the auditor • Date of the auditor's report • Auditor's address	• Auditor concludes from evidence obtained that financial statements are not free from material misstatement. • Auditor is unable to obtain sufficient appropriate audit evidence to conclude the financial statements are free from material misstatement.	No material misstatement – unmodified report. Material – "Except for" qualification for both misstatement and lack of evidence. Material and pervasive – • adverse opinion (for a misstatement) • disclaimer opinion (for a lack of evidence).
Detail chapter 9.3 and 9.4		On what grounds is an audit report qualified?	Detail chapter 9.6 to 9.8

ISA 706 Modified / unqualified reports   ISA 710 Comparative information

What types of modified / unqualified reports are there?	What are the examples of emphasis of matter paragraphs?	What are the auditor's responsibilities regarding comparative information?	So when does the auditor have to report?
• Emphasis of matter – referring to matters in the financial statements. • Other matters – anything else that the auditor wishes to bring to the attention of the users of the financial statements.	• Uncertainties on the outcome of litigation. • Early application of an accounting standard. • Ongoing major disasters affecting a company.	• Obtain sufficient appropriate evidence to ensure that comparative information is presented according to the applicable financial reporting framework. • Report in accordance with the auditor's reporting responsibilities.	The auditor will *normally* report where: • the prior year's audit report was qualified and the matter is unresolved • audit evidence obtained this year suggested material misstatement in corresponding figures • prior year financial statements audited by another auditor • corresponding amounts not audited.
Detail chapter 9.5		Detail chapter 9.9	

ISA 720 Other information

How can other information differ from the audited financial statements?	What does the auditor do if other information is different from audited information?
• Inconsistent – other information contradicts or is different from the audited financial statements. • Misstatements of fact – other information does not appear in the financial statements – but it is incorrect.	Assuming that the financial statements and/or other information are not changed, then actions are: • other information is correct – qualify opinion on the financial statements • financial statements are correct – issue an "other matter" paragraph.

Detail chapter 9.10

Chapter 11
Index

A student's guide to Auditing By Alan Lewin

705 Modifications to the opinion in the independent auditor's report 269

H

I

M

N

O